# THE LIFE AND MINISTRY
## OF JESUS

# THE LIFE AND
# MINISTRY OF JESUS

BY

VINCENT TAYLOR

D.D.

LONDON

MACMILLAN & CO LTD

1954

MACMILLAN AND COMPANY LIMITED
*London Bombay Calcutta Madras Melbourne*

THE MACMILLAN COMPANY OF CANADA LIMITED
*Toronto*

ST MARTIN'S PRESS INC
*New York*

PRINTED IN GREAT BRITAIN

# PREFACE

THIS book is an enlarged version of the Second Series of Speaker's Lectures on the Person of Christ in New Testament Teaching delivered at Oxford during the years 1952–3. It has a comparatively long history behind it. As far back as 1942 I began to feel that Christology cannot be effectively studied unless we can give an intelligible account of the life and ministry of Jesus as they are revealed in the Gospels. I therefore took the opportunity offered by a request from the Editors of the *Interpreter's Bible*, published by the Abingdon-Cokesbury Press, Nashville, New York, to write a short sketch entitled 'The Life and Ministry of Jesus', and this study was printed in 1951 in Volume 7 of that commentary. The publishers graciously permitted me to expand this article, and I cannot be too grateful to them for this kindness, for it has enabled me to re-examine many of the ideas originally put forward and to supplement the treatment given in various ways. On important matters I have not found reason to alter the opinions first expressed, but further study and the discipline of delivering lectures at Oxford and at University College, Cardiff, have enabled me to add many important points of detail and to present the subject more broadly and coherently. I have also taken the opportunity to add a section called 'Prolegomena', in which I discuss the sources of our knowledge of Jesus, their historical value, and the relationship between the Jesus of history and the Christ of faith.

Any one who attempts to write a Life of Christ must

recognise from the outset that his task will end in failure, greater or less as the case may be, and that he must be ready to face failure in his endeavour to see the historic Jesus more clearly. In part the difficulty of the task is due to the fragmentary character of the sources. Apart from isolated notices in Josephus, Tacitus, and Suetonius, and late traditions in the Talmud, the available evidence is limited to the four Gospels and the Epistles. As mentioned already, the historical value of the Gospels will be discussed later. Here it is enough to say that their testimony ranges from excellent historical traditions, based ultimately upon eyewitnesses, to secondary narratives which are coloured by later Christian beliefs, and that, in consequence, in using them it is necessary to apply to their evaluation the accepted principles of literary and historical criticism, sometimes to make conjectures, and even to essay the use of a scientific imagination controlled by facts. At a hundred points, therefore, the writer's results will be open to question, and in the end he may satisfy no one, for, while some degree of selection is possible, he must consider all the disputed points that arise. He cannot emulate the example of Prince George of Denmark, the husband of Queen Anne, who was wont to greet difficult political events as they emerged with the remark, 'Is it possible?'. The nature of the sources, however, is not the main difficulty which confronts the would-be historian, for there are many great figures of the past, notably Socrates, for the knowledge of whose life and teaching we have much less and much inferior evidence. The greater problem is to do justice to the place of Jesus on the field of human history and to the creative influence he has exercised upon the faith, devotion, and worship of the Church throughout the centuries, and to attempt to do these things without allowing bias injuriously to influence one's estimation of the significance of the original tradition. The reader can be trusted to distinguish personal opinions, which after many years of study and reflection may not be without force, from well based historical inferences and conclusions. In the story of Jesus many things are mysterious and some problems are insoluble. The test to be applied to honest attempts to relate that story are fidelity in the interpretation of the sources and a full appreciation of the wonder and greatness of Jesus.

It should be explained that many of the passages of Scripture are taken from the Revised Standard Version of the Bible copyrighted 1946 and 1952, and are used by courtesy of Thomas Nelson & Sons Limited, Edinburgh. For this permission I am grateful.

I desire also to express my gratitude to my friends, the Rev. Dr. C. L. Mitton and the Rev. Dr. A. J. B. Higgins, for their valuable help in correcting the proofs, and to the printers for their great skill and accuracy.

VINCENT TAYLOR

# CONTENTS

## PROLEGOMENA

## PART I: THE PERIOD BEFORE THE GALILEAN MINISTRY

## PART II: THE GALILEAN MINISTRY

## PART III: THE WITHDRAWAL FROM GALILEE

## PART IV: THE JERUSALEM MINISTRY

PART V: THE PASSION AND RESURRECTION

## ABBREVIATIONS

ET   = *The Expository Times.*

JTS  = *The Journal of Theological Studies.*

KThW = *Theologisches Wörterbuch zum Neuen Testament* (ed. G. Kittel).

L    = The special Lukan (Caesarean) tradition.

LQR  = *The London Quarterly and Holborn Review.*

M    = A source containing sayings and parables used by Matthew.

Q    = The sayings-source used in common by Matthew and Luke.

RSV  = The Revised Standard Version.

RV   = The Revised Version.

VGT  = *The Vocabulary of the Greek Testament,* J. H. Moulton and G. Milligan.

# PROLEGOMENA

# I

## THE POSSIBILITY OF WRITING
## A LIFE OF CHRIST

**M**ANY scholars believe that the attempt to write a Life of Christ is so difficult as to be almost impossible. This opinion has steadily grown since the publication of Schweitzer's *Quest of the Historical Jesus* (Eng. Tr. 1910) and still more since the rise of Form Criticism a generation ago. In consequence, the earlier veritable spate of historical studies has given place to a slow stream and recently to a mere trickle.

Form Criticism is by no means the only influence which has created this situation. It is well known that the late Canon William Sanday, perhaps the most outstanding British New Testament scholar of his day, passed away in 1920 'without having written a page of what was to have been the great work of his life, a critical life of Christ',[1] and Professor Goguel[2] has told us that the same is true of the two great Roman Catholic scholars, L. de Grandmaison and M.-J. Lagrange. Lagrange, he reminds us, wrote concerning the four Gospels, 'They form the only *Life of Jesus* which can be written; all we have to do is to understand them'. There can be no doubt that a potent cause leading to the decline of biographical works of the kind is the range and complexity of the critical issues involved, including Textual problems, Synoptic Criticism, the question of the Fourth Gospel, the Virgin Birth, the problem of miracles, and the modern emphasis upon

---

[1] Cf. A. Plummer, *The Expository Times*, xxxii, 151f.
[2] *The Life of Jesus* (Eng. Tr. 1933), 60.

3

eschatology. But the more important restraining influence is the difficulty of presenting a life of Christ which is at once critical and yet coherent with the Christology of the Creeds. Sanday's *Christologies Ancient and Modern* (1910) and his essay *Personality in Christ and in Ourselves* (1911) reveal how keenly he was alive to this problem.[1]

Form Criticism has greatly accentuated the hazard of writing a life of Christ, especially its basic assumptions that in the primitive Church the tradition consisted of a mass of isolated units and that, as we now find it in the Gospels, it is strongly coloured and shaped by doctrinal beliefs. It is not surprising that the leading Form Critics think the historical task is a vain undertaking. In his book, *Jesus* (1926), Bultmann wrote, 'I do indeed think that we can now know almost nothing concerning the life and personality of Jesus, since the early Christian sources show no interest in either, are moreover fragmentary and often legendary; and other sources about Jesus do not exist'.[2] G. Bertram also has said, 'The figure of Jesus is not directly accessible to history. It is futile to try to place him within a process of historical development . . .; not what he was, but what he is, is all that is revealed to the believer; the historian must be content with this statement'.[3] In close agreement with the principles of Form Criticism the words with which K. L. Schmidt ended his *Der Rahmen der Geschichte Jesu* (1919) have made a deep impression upon the minds of

[1] See *Christology and Personality* (1911) which includes the two works. In the Preface Sanday wrote, 'I hope this is the last of the preliminary studies which I have found myself compelled to make in approaching the larger task which lies before me of writing, or attempting to write, what is commonly called a Life of Christ', p. v.

[2] Cited from the English translation, *Jesus and the Word*, 8, made by Louise Pettibone Smith and Erminie Huntress.

[3] *Neues Testament und historische Methode*, 1928, p. 41. Cited by Goguel, *op. cit.*, 59.

New Testament scholars: 'The stories of Jesus lie for the most part on one and the same plane. Only now and then, from considerations about the inner character of a story, can we fix these somewhat more precisely in respect of time and place. But as a whole, there is no Life of Christ in the sense of an evolving biography, no chronological sketch of the Story of Jesus, but only single narratives, sections, which are put into a framework'.[1] One cannot be surprised that a kind of intellectual paralysis fell upon attempts to record the Story. When, for example, Professor S. J. Case, of Chicago, wrote his *Jesus—A New Biography* (1927), he renounced the attempt to give a detailed sketch of events, and concentrated his attention on the task and the religion of Jesus, judging every statement in the records by the degree of its suitableness to his distinctive environment and to that of those who framed the Gospel tradition in the history of Christianity. This project was symptomatic. Many scholars, and not only those who accept the more extreme results of Form Criticism, view with dubiety attempts to undertake constructive presentations.

The historical character of the Gospel tradition is considered later.[2] It is no doubt upon that particular issue that the question turns whether, even if a biography is impossible, a sketch of the life of Jesus is not a vain undertaking.

The history of criticism itself seems to me to give grounds for greater courage. Even if the opinion were better based than it is, that the Gospels merely reflect the beliefs of the second and third generations of the first Christians, it would still be incumbent upon us to ask what these beliefs imply concerning Jesus and the purposes of his ministry; and it is significant that Bultmann

[1] *Op. cit.*, 317.    [2] See pp. 25–34.

himself made such an attempt in his *Jesus*. Much more justifiable must a constructive purpose appear to those who, while appreciative of the many insights of Form Critics, cannot accept their extreme views.

In English-speaking countries 'the cast iron Markan hypothesis' never had the currency it enjoyed in Germany, and it has been felt that, while K. L. Schmidt has shown that the Markan outline is much looser than had been supposed, it 'does represent a genuine succession of events, within which movement and development can be traced'. These are the words of C. H. Dodd in an important article, 'The Framework of the Gospel Narrative', in the *Expository Times* (xliii, 396–400), and similar views have been expressed by F. C. Burkitt,[1] W. F. Howard,[2] and others.

In 1941–2 the question, 'Is it possible to write a Life of Christ?', was discussed in detail in three articles in the *Expository Times*. In one of them Dr. C. J. Cadoux concluded his discussion by saying: 'I do not concur in the modern view that it is impossible to write a life of Christ, though I recognise that any such life must suffer from the limitation and peculiar character of the records'. 'If such a life is ever written', he added, 'it will inevitably bring with it a few painful surprises; but these will be more than off-set by the added clearness with which we shall see the real Jesus'.[3] These opinions found expression in his *Historic Mission of Jesus* (1941) and in his stimulating *Life of Jesus* (1948) in the Pelican Series. A cautious but affirmative answer was also given by Professor T. W. Manson in a further article. 'We have not enough material', he wrote, 'for a biography of Jesus, nor

---

[1] *The Journal of Theological Studies*, xxxvi. 187f.
[2] *The London Quarterly Review* (July, 1927), 79.
[3] Vol. liii. 175–7.

even for a complete narrative of the ministry. The materials at our disposal are, however, sufficient for a more limited enterprise. We can set the ministry in its historical context: we can read the history of post-exilic Judaism forward to the critical point; and we can read the history of the Early Church backwards to the same critical point'. He went on to say that we can describe with fair accuracy the most important factors of the total situation and measure more or less exactly the tensions which made the Cross inevitable. 'And having got these things', he continued, 'we can give some kind of outline of the events that led up to the Cross; and as we apply our best scholarship and insight, sympathy, and sincerity to these various tasks, we may hope that the portrait of Jesus will emerge with some sufficient clearness'.[1] This judgement was subsequently illustrated by Professor Manson in a succession of important articles in the *Bulletin of the John Rylands Library*[2] and in his *The Servant-Messiah: A Study of the Public Ministry of Jesus* (1953).

Of special interest in this connexion is Professor Goguel's *Life of Jesus* (Eng. Tr. 1933). In this work use is made not only of the Synoptic Gospels, but also of traditions implied in the Fourth Gospel. Goguel maintains that the Pauline theology, 'the most ancient form of Christianity to which we have direct access', 'witnesses to the existence of an historical tradition about Jesus without which it would be inexplicable',[3] and he quotes the opinion of Renan that there is sufficient material in the Epistles to construct a 'small *Life of Jesus*'.[4] Goguel recognises that

---

[1] Vol. liii. 251. In a third article in the same Series (*ET*, liii. 60–5) an affirmative answer is also given by the present writer.

[2] Vols. xxvii (1943), 323–7, xxxii (1950), 171–93, xxxiii (1951), 271–82.

[3] *Op. cit.*, 115.                    [4] *Op. cit.*, 119.

all Lives of Jesus will lack that solid scaffolding which supports and holds together the effort to read the story of the past, and admits that a large element of conjecture is inevitable, but says that, for the historian, 'the main lines of the life of Jesus are clear'.[1]

Among less ambitious but suggestive books which illustrate the conviction that a Life of Christ is possible may be mentioned Professor A. M. Hunter's *Work and Words of Jesus* (1950) and Dr. R. Dunkerley's *Hope of Jesus: A Study in Moral Eschatology* (1953). It would appear that we are entering upon a period of greater constructive activity.

It is not suggested that the opinions and the works mentioned above decisively answer the question under discussion, but undoubtedly they point to a different climate from that of historical pessimism. And each has a significance which extends beyond itself; they give expression to the conviction that any just appreciation of Christ's person and of his place in theology and religious experience must be based on his teaching and the facts of his earthly life. C. J. Cadoux[2] rightly recalls the wise words of Canon R. C. Moberly: 'Councils, we admit, and Creeds cannot go behind, but must wholly rest upon the history of our Lord Jesus Christ'.[3] Despite the increased complexity of the question of Gospel origins, there is no discharge from this principle. The Catholic faith rests upon Scripture, and what Christ did and taught is a fundamental concern of doctrine. It is time to cease girding at the older liberals, whose greatness, like good wine, needs no bush. If we do not like their constructions, we must take over their business under new management, for to attempt to expound

---

[1] *Op. cit.*, 213.    [2] *The Historic Mission of Jesus*, 336.
[3] *Lux Mundi* (1890 ed.), 243.

doctrine without a scrupulous regard for the truth of the
Gospel tradition is to build upon sand. Since Christology
is inalienably bound up with history, we must descend to
the basement and beneath to its foundations, even though
the glory of the temple of faith is seen only from the skies.
Whether a sketch of the life and ministry of Jesus is
possible depends on our sources and their historical value,
and to these questions we now turn.

# II

## THE SOURCES

### I

I BEGIN with the Two-document Hypothesis, the view that Mark and the sayings-source Q were used by Matthew and Luke in addition to oral tradition. In the words of Dibelius this hypothesis 'is still the sure foundation of the criticism of the Synoptics',[1] in spite, we may add, of a recent tendency to speak disparagingly of 'the hypothetical Q' and the forthright attack upon it by B. C. Butler in *The Originality of St. Matthew* (1951).[2] The Abbot of Downside has thrown into the melting-pot not only the Q hypothesis, but also the priority of Mark and the independence in origin of Matthew and Luke, thus reviving the ancient, but now generally discredited, view that Matthew is the original Gospel. The new *Catholic Commentary on Holy Scripture* (1953), which illustrates the emphasis which the Church of Rome is laying upon the importance of the Bible, significantly modifies the traditional hypothesis by the view, advocated by Père Benoit, that Q is the original Aramaic Gospel of Matthew translated into Greek and used as a source by the three Synoptists.[3] Misgivings regarding Q have been

---

[1] *The Expository Times*, xli. 537.

[2] Abbot Butler describes Q as 'an unnecessary and vicious hypothesis', *op. cit.*, 170.

[3] Cf. also Dr. Alfred Wikenhauser, *Einleitung in das Neue Testament*, (1953), 162–82, who affirms that the Greek Matthew and Luke are both dependent on Mark, and suggests that Matthew composed the *logia* in Aramaic, the Greek translation being the common source (Q) used in the

expressed by C. K. Barrett[1] and more trenchantly by Dr. Austin Farrer in *A Study in Mark*.[2]

## II

Abbot Butler's submissions are difficult to answer just because of their comprehensive character. In the history of Synoptic Criticism the priority of Mark and the mutual independence of Matthew and Luke were affirmed before the Q hypothesis was advanced. To reject all three hypotheses together is therefore to return to the position as it obtained a century ago when the Synoptic problem was in the greatest confusion. That is why Abbot Butler's case, even when felt to be unconvincing, is not easy to refute. It is necessary to disentangle the problems, and to begin where criticism began, with the priority of Mark.

It is here that Butler fails. He makes skilful play with the incautious claim of many that Lachmann held the priority of Mark, but neglects the fact that Lachmann claimed that the basic Synoptic order is reflected best in Mark. This was the determinative observation, and from it the rest followed. The strong arguments on which the priority of Mark, in substantially its existing form, are based, the common order, the many stylistic variants in the later Gospels, the manner in which its bolder statements are modified, and the legendary character of the special Matthaean tradition,[3] are conclusive. Mark is the primary source.[4]

Greek Matthew and Luke. See the review of G. D. Kilpatrick, *Journal of Theological Studies*, N.S., iv. 228f.

[1] *The Expository Times*, liv. 320–3.

[2] *Op. cit.*, 210.

[3] It is not enough at this time of the day to say, as Butler does, 'We deny that they (the narratives peculiar to Mt.) are legendary accretions of a period subsequent to Mark's composition', *op. cit.*, 164.

[4] See the important article of Dr. H. G. Wood, 'The Priority of Mark', *Expository Times*, lxv. 17–19.

No more convincing is the alleged dependence of Luke on Matthew. As the fathers of Synoptic criticism found a century ago, no final conclusion is possible so long as the discussion is limited to the comparison of parallel passages. The vital arguments are the patent differences in the two Gospels in the Birth Stories and the Passion Narratives, the want of the special Matthaean tradition in Luke, and the fact that the two Evangelists never agree against Mark in the order of their narratives.

### III

The strong case for the Q Hypothesis emerges only when the priority of Mark and the independence of Luke are recognised. The relevant points are the high percentage of agreement between Matthew and Luke in non-Markan contexts, the striking agreement in the order of the sayings in the two Gospels, the existence of doublets, one member of which is manifestly taken from Mark. These points, except a dubious explanation of the doublets,[1] do not appear in Butler's polemical volume. Q is dismissed without being attacked and the trumpets sound before the citadel is taken.

Here I may be permitted to mention an investigation of my own recorded in the *Journal of Theological Studies*.[2] The lists of parallel passages in Matthew and Luke usually displayed in two columns are not too impressive. A common order is suggested, but there are so many exceptions that what ought to be a telling argument too often has the appearance of an apology. The case is very different, however, if we leave out of account some 44 verses, in which it is possible that Matthew conflates Q with another source, and then set out the remaining 200

---

[1] They are attributed to Matthew's editorial repetition, *op. cit.*, 145.

[2] 'The Order of Q', iv. (NS), 27–31.

verses, not in two columns, but in seven; with Luke on the left and with Matthew in six columns, including the five blocks of sayings-material in v-vii, x, xiii, xviii, xxiii-v, and in the rest of that Gospel. The results are startling. With the exception of some 10 sayings, in which editorial re-arrangement on the part of either Evangelist is to be suspected, the passages follow in common sequences visible to the eye. There can be no objection to the current practice of speaking of Q as 'a hypothetical source', since we do not possess it in its original form, but let us have done with the apologetic tone in which that phrase is used, as if the hypothesis were somewhat dubious. There are very cogent reasons for affirming that, in addition to their use of Mark, Matthew and Luke drew upon a common source Q, which consisted mainly of sayings. In the pre-Gospel period it was a Greek document. Probably at an earlier time it was current in Aramaic, and it may have been a combination of older collections or groups of sayings and parables, but there is no reason to doubt that Matthew and Luke used a written non-Markan collection.

IV

Streeter's Four-document Hypothesis is an extension of the Two-document Hypothesis advanced to explain facts not otherwise covered. The view that Matthew used a source M, consisting of sayings and parables, has much in its favour, although from the nature of the case, it must be a more speculative entity than Q. The suggestion that Luke used L, a document containing narratives, parables and sayings, has a long history behind it.[1] In Streeter's opinion Luke combined L with Q to form

1 Cf. V. Taylor, *Behind the Third Gospel*, 2–27.

Proto-Luke or, in more scientific terminology, Q + L¹ and whatever may be thought of the more picturesque accounts of the Proto-Luke Hypothesis, there is good reason to think that Q + L existed before his Gospel was written.² It may well be that L was an oral source, and that the theory with a future is a Three-document Hypothesis which posits the use of Mark, Q, and M, supplemented by oral sources in the L tradition, the Birth Stories of Luke, and the narratives peculiar to Matthew. Documentary hypotheses are not likely to be abandoned, but it is probable that all the Evangelists, including the Fourth Evangelist, have drawn upon oral tradition to a greater extent than has been commonly recognised. The preface to Luke, with its reference to many who had already undertaken the compilation of narratives (i. 1), points to the existence of documentary sources, but its further allusion to eyewitnesses and ministers of the Word (i. 2) suggests, what is otherwise probable in itself, that oral tradition was also available to those who compiled Gospels (i. 3) for the primitive communities, whereby men might know the truth concerning the things in which they had been instructed (i. 4).

V

There is another meaning to the word 'sources' which is of essential importance to the historian. The sources described above are those used by the Evangelists, and the modern critic cannot afford to neglect them; but in constructive work his sources are also the Gospels themselves, with all the light they reflect from the circumstances and conditions in which they were written. Be-

¹ *The Four Gospels*, 199–222.
² Cf. J. W. Hunkin, *The Journal of Theological Studies*, April, 1927, 250–62, also *The New Testament: A Conspectus* (1950), 78.

hind the Gospels is the many-sided life of the Church,
which defended itself against attack, instructed its
catechumens, shaped its liturgy, and formulated its
doctrine.   It is for this reason that Form Criticism is so
important.   Despite its aberrations, its necessarily speculative character, and the sceptical tendencies of many of its
exponents, its suggestions regarding the *Sitz im Leben*
of the various items of the Gospel tradition and the early
formation of the Passion Narrative can be of the greatest
value to the historian who seeks to raise the curtain which
otherwise hides from our eyes the life and ministry of
Jesus.   The Gospels are the source of our knowledge of
him, but the Gospels as interpreted and understood.

# III

## THE MATERIAL CONTAINED
## IN THE FOUR GOSPELS

IN this section questions of introduction, of author-
ship, date, and the like, will not be discussed, but the
material the Gospels contain and the manner in which
it has been used by the Evangelists.

I

I begin with the Gospel of Mark. It is still true to say
that, except by the most radical critics, the historical value
of this Gospel is highly esteemed. Mark must always
remain our primary authority for our knowledge of the
ministry of Jesus. This opinion, however, cannot be
extended to cover everything recorded in Mark, for the
excellent reason that its outline is broken and the material
it contains is not all of one mould. Many of its narratives
reflect the testimony of eyewitnesses, but others are
popular stories from which by a process of attrition much
of the narrative element has fallen away, while others
again are 'constructions' in which fragmentary tradition
has been pieced together by the Evangelist. The Passion
Narrative in Mark is the expansion of an earlier account
by the use of the best tradition, and throughout the Gospel
excerpts are introduced from what appears to have been
an early collection of sayings which is independent of Q.
Various influences, apologetic, catechetical, liturgical, and
doctrinal, have left their impress upon the Markan
tradition, but we ought not to regard their results as the
corruption of an earlier perfect record, for there never was

such a record, but rather as windows through which we can still read the history of transmission in the earliest days. These influences are especially important in connexion with such narratives as the Transfiguration, the nature miracles, and the visit of the women to the Empty Tomb. These questions, and many others, are discussed in my commentary, *The Gospel according to St. Mark*. Here I can only repeat my conviction that Mark is a writing of first-rate historical importance.

II

The value of the Gospel of Luke depends mainly upon the fidelity with which the Third Evangelist has reproduced the sayings of Jesus from Q and upon his use of the narratives and parables of the L tradition. L is at least as early as Mark, but its narratives are less detailed and less vivid. In some of them there is a tendency for details from one story to pass over into another as in the Call of the First Disciples in v. 1–11 (cf. Mk. i. 16–20) and the account of the Woman in the City who was a Sinner in vii. 36–50 (cf. Mk. xiv. 3–9). Of special interest and importance is the Lukan Passion Narrative, on which criticism has by no means said its last word.

Something must be said of Luke's 'artistry'. Almost half a century ago V. H. Stanton,[1] of Cambridge, carefully examined the Evangelist's literary style, and came to the conclusion that in nine sections the form of the narratives is due solely to the author himself. These sections include the two narratives[2] mentioned above, the Ministering Women (viii. 1–3), the parable of the Good Samaritan (x. 29–37), the Ten Lepers (xvii. 11–19), the Lament over Jerusalem (xix. 41–44), the Trial before

[1] *The Gospels as Historical Documents*, ii. (1909), 291–312.
[2] Lk. v. 1–11 and vii. 36–50.

Herod (xxiii. 5–12, 14f.), the Penitent Thief (xxiii. 39–43), and the Appearances of the Risen Christ (xxiv). In these sections Luke displays his inspired artistry in transcribing the oral traditions to which he had access. Opinions must necessarily vary regarding the historical bearings of his literary activity. For my own part I believe that his work is mainly interpretative and that, with general fidelity to the tradition as a whole, he felt himself at liberty to use his imagination to the full in depicting these sublime scenes. Resting on a factual basis now beyond recovery, they are to be estimated as works of art rather than more sober reports and are to be welcomed as setting before us the person of Jesus dramatically in a picturesque form.

The case is rather different in the Birth Stories of Lk. i and ii. Here the Evangelist's art is exercised to a greater degree. There are scholars who trace these narratives to the Virgin Mary and the women who are traditionally associated with her in view of such passages as ii. 19, 'But Mary kept all these things, pondering them in her heart', but, it must be confessed, the evidence is of the slenderest character. It is surely better to conclude that, using the Virgin Birth tradition, Luke freely composed a dramatic story imaginatively coloured and deliberately expressed in the vocabulary, style, and ideas of the Septuagint. And in part we can see how he has done this. If we compare the stories in the parallel cycles concerning John the Baptist and Jesus, we find that the words characteristic of the Evangelist are *below* the average in the Baptist cycle, but *above* the average in the Jesus cycle in the stories of the Annunciation (i. 26–38), the Visit of Mary to Elisabeth (i. 39–45, 56), and in many of those in Lk. ii. The natural inference is that Luke found the John cycle already in existence in a Hebrew or Aramaic source, and used it as a model in constructing the Birth Stories of Jesus. If this is so, the narratives are not historical in the narrower sense of the term, although they are of great value to the theologian as reflecting the estimate of an early Palestinian community regarding the divinity of Christ. The historian should take off his shoes because the ground is holy, but he must lay down his pen if he seeks to relate sober history. The ultimate question is theological.[1]

In thinking of this special element in Luke we are in danger of seeing the whole out of perspective. Wherever Luke has a source at his disposal, he follows it closely. He often alters the beginning and the end of a Markan narrative and effects other literary and editorial changes,[2] but beyond introducing words and constructions of his own, he retains the body of the original. The same is true of his use of Q,[3] and in Acts i-xv he often sacrifices style to the preservation of the rough Greek rendering of an Aramaic source. We are entitled to regard the Gospel as a primary authority which, with the reservations made, reproduces the earliest tradition.

This conclusion is particularly valuable in view of the Evangelist's special interests in the poor, the outcasts, Samaritans, women, social relationships, and teaching about prayer, joy, and the Holy Spirit. If he emphasises the universality of the Gospel, he is only bringing out its implications, and over-emphasis in this matter can be corrected by reference to the other sources. The broad

---

[1] The theological issue is whether the coming of the Son of God into the world entailed a mode of entrance other than that of ordinary generation. Cf. O.C. Quick, *Doctrines of the Creed*, 156–61.

[2] Cf. H. J. Cadbury, *The Style and Literary Method of Luke*, 1920, 105–19.

[3] Cf. Cadbury, *op. cit.*, 124–6. 'But the words of Jesus themselves, the *verba ipsissima*, whether reported by Mark or found in the source designated Q, have rarely been retouched by the author of the third Gospel to give them a wider scope of application', *op. cit.*, 124.

humanity of his Gospel in the immortal parables of the Lost Coin, the Lost Son, the Good Samaritan, the Friend at Midnight , the Unjust Judge, and the Pharisee and the Publican remind us of how much would be wanting if we did not possess this Gospel.[1]

### III

From the historical point of view the main value of Matthew is that it is another witness to the teaching of Q and that it alone draws upon the sayings and parables of M. The Evangelist's use of Mark raises many problems, especially when in obedience to later interests the bolder statements of his source are softened and secondary tradition is added. The narrative element peculiar to Matthew is the least valuable part of the Synoptic tradition. In it the beginnings of Christian legend are visible, in the apologetic stories of Mt. i and ii, in the account of Peter walking on the water, and the additions to the Markan Passion Narrative, the Pilate stories, the earthquake and the resurrection of the saints, the guard at the tomb, and the descent of the angel at the Resurrection. These are the stories which provide unbelief with its sharpest stones and Hollywood with its brightest inspirations.

Again, as in the case of Luke, this part of the tradition must not be allowed to throw the greatness of Matthew out of focus. The writer reflects special interests in the fulfilment of prophecy, apocalyptic, and the Church, and except in sayings from the M source, in the universality of the Gentile Mission. There is in Matthew a greater

[1] In his penetrating study of the parables Jeremias observes that, apart from existing expressions and verses which are taken over, the extensive parabolic material peculiar to Luke contains, so far as he can see, no examples of allegorical interpretation, cf. *Die Gleichnisse Jesu*, 68

interpretative element than in Mark and Luke, although
it is smaller in extent and less doctrinal than that present
in John.   Interpretation, however, is not necessarily
perversion; it may bring out implications in the tradition
lost in more purely factual records.  The student of the
Gospels has to enlarge his conceptions of historical
portraiture in order to include much more than the statements of colourless records.  This discipline is particularly
necessary in any attempt to see the Gospels in their true
historical setting and to use them for constructive
purposes.

IV

We turn, lastly, to the Fourth Gospel.  In this Gospel
interpretation is manifest to a superlative degree.  This
fact has repeatedly been illustrated in the discussions of
the last three decades, and especially by C. H. Dodd in his
*Interpretation of the Fourth Gospel* (1953).  Professor Dodd
says that he regards the Gospel as being in its essential
character a theological work rather than a history, but
immediately points out that the writer has chosen to set
forth his theology under the literary form of a 'Gospel',
that is, a recital of the historical narrative of the sufferings,
death, and resurrection of Jesus Christ, prefaced by some
account of his ministry in word and deed.[1]  The Evangelist himself describes his purpose when he writes, 'These
are written, that you may believe that Jesus is the Christ,
the Son of God; and that in believing you may have life
in his name' (xx. 31).  In the light of this statement there
can be no doubt that his supreme aim is to bring out the
significance of the events and of the person he describes,
and there is good reason to infer that he does this in terms
of Hellenistic thought and the Rabbinical speculations of

---

[1] *Op. cit.*, 444

his day. Those old-fashioned second century Christians described by Epiphanius as 'the Alogi', and by Irenaeus as 'wretched men' who 'do not admit that aspect presented by John's Gospel, in which the Lord promised that he would send the Paraclete', were keen sighted enough to perceive this element in the Fourth Gospel, although its historical roots were hidden from them. The problem of to-day is whether we can combine the insight of the Alogi with the one-sided affirmations of Irenaeus. Is the Fourth Gospel a legitimate interpretation of the primitive tradition? That it is an interpretation can hardly be in doubt.

We consider first the narratives in the Gospel. Those which are based upon the Synoptic tradition, as, for example, the Feeding of the Five Thousand and the Anointing at Bethany, reveal fidelity to that tradition coupled with a manifest design to bring out the doctrinal aspects of the incidents. And we may well believe that other narratives, not represented in the Synoptic Gospels, are based on special traditions known to the Evangelist. But it is doubtful if we can carry through this argument in respect of all the Johannine stories, for scenes are depicted, as in the conversation with the woman of Samaria and the examination before Pilate, when no eyewitness was present[1] and the suggestion that Jesus told his disciples of them can be no more than a surmise. We are bound to recognise that the Evangelist dramatises incidents in order to bring out their doctrinal significance, picturing events as they were visible, after years of reflection, to the eyes of faith, and that often we cannot be certain of the form of the tradition with which he began. Obviously, in the Fourth Gospel a new form of historical tradition presents itself, and the problem of the modern reader is

[1] Cf. Dodd, *op. cit.*, 450.

whether he can accompany the Evangelist with understanding on his inspired flight.

The sayings have the same character as the narratives.
Many of them, far more than is commonly supposed, are
Synoptic sayings expressed in the Evangelist's idiom;[1]
others are non-Synoptic sayings, similarly re-phrased,
which came to the Evangelist in other ways.   Even the
Paraclete sayings in xiv-xvi have a lineal connexion with
the sayings on confessing, denying, and being ashamed of
Christ in Mk. viii. 38 and in Lk. xii. 8f. = Mt. x. 32f.,[2]
and the commission to remit sins in Jn. xx. 23 is a recast
of the sayings on binding and loosing in Mt. xvi. 19 and
xviii. 18 under the influence of the ecclesiastical situation
of the Evangelist's day.   I doubt, however, if we have all
the facts before us unless we recognise that in other
sayings, of which those concerning the Father and the Son
in v. 19–29 and those in the high priestly prayer in xvii
are conspicuous examples, the Evangelist himself unfolds
what he believes to be, under the guidance of the Holy
Spirit (cf. xvi. 13), the mind of Christ.   There is a
parallel in Browning's words, often quoted in this
connexion to-day, in which the poet refers to his use of
*The Old Yellow Book* in *The Ring and the Book*,[3] and says
that it contains

> 'Something of mine, which, mixed up with the mass,
> Made it bear hammer and be firm to file'.

What, then, are we to say of the historical value of the
Fourth Gospel?   Little indeed, if we will have it that the
historical is the purely factual, but much if we believe that

---

[1] Cf. W. F. Howard, *The Fourth Gospel in Recent Criticism and Interpretation*, 215–29.

[2] Cf. H. Windisch, *Die fünf johanneischen Parakletsprüche, Festgabe
für Adolf Jülicher*, 1927, 125.

[3] I. 462f.

interpretation is a valid form of historical writing, and that
the Evangelist's work is legitimate interpretation. That
his interpretation is legitimate, as compared, say, with
the fantastic developments in the Apocryphal Gospels, is
shown by three things: (1) our knowledge of the Synoptic
sayings with which he so often begins, (2) the many
points of contact between the picture of the Johannine
Christ and that presented by the Synoptists, and (3) the
response his interpretation has evoked throughout the
centuries, so that many Christians find themselves
peculiarly 'at home' with John, while appreciative of the
worth of the Synoptics and the Pauline Epistles as a whole.[1]
To these considerations we may add the special Johannine
traditions which historians of the calibre of Goguel[2]
believe to be historical, such as the tradition concerning a
pre-Galilean ministry, the extended treatment given to
the Jerusalem ministry, the references to Annas, the date
of the Last Supper, and the strong emphasis laid upon
the reality of the humanity of Jesus, the divine Word who
became flesh. One cannot hesitate to affirm that the
Fourth Gospel contributes to a fuller appreciation of
Jesus and his teaching than can be gained from the
Synoptic Gospels read in isolation.

[1] Cf. W. Temple, *Readings in St. John*, p. v.
[2] *The Life of Jesus*, 150–7, 405–25.

# IV

## THE HISTORICAL VALUE
## OF THE GOSPEL TRADITION

FROM the sources of the Gospels and the Evangelist's use of different kinds of material we now turn to the vital question of the Gospel tradition. Is the tradition a reliable guide to the investigation of the mind and purpose of Jesus?

In this connexion the closing words of R. H. Lightfoot in his *History and Interpretation in the Gospels* (1935) have frequently been quoted:

'It seems, then, that the form of the earthly no less than of the heavenly Christ is for the most part hidden from us. For all the inestimable value of the gospels, they yield us little more than a whisper of his voice; we trace in them but the outskirts of his ways. Only when we see him hereafter in his fulness shall we know him as he was on earth'.[1]

Many readers read these words with dismay and some with a mournful acquiescence in their truth.

Recently, in his *Gospel Message of St. Mark* (1951) Professor Lightfoot referred to what he called a widespread misunderstanding of this passage. He pointed out that it contains almost a quotation of Job xxvi. 14, and observed that the patriarch would have been even more grievously distressed than he already was, if he had thought that his words would be taken to imply that he had practically no knowledge of his God. This explanation must be accepted, but one may doubt if it meets the real difficulty. We must therefore ask whether the more

---

[1] *Op. cit.*, 225.

radical interpretation of the passage represents the facts. Is it only 'a whisper of his voice' that we hear in the Gospel tradition?

This inquiry is the more necessary in view of what H. E. W. Turner describes as 'the mood of historical pessimism which has come of late years over historical criticism'.[1] Echoes of the views of Bultmann and Bertram, to which reference has already been made, and of the scepticism of Loisy[2] and Guignebert,[3] can be heard in Great Britain and America. A gap, it is pointed out, amounting to a generation separates Mark from the ministry of Jesus, and even if it is allowed that Q may be dated about A.D. 50, there is still an interval of about twenty years from the original facts. It is not possible, it is argued, to get behind the primary sources; we can only examine what the Evangelists tell us, recognising that they wrote against the background of the religious ideas of their day.

This scepticism seems to me excessive; it arises from too docile an acceptance of the more radical views of Form Critics. Several considerations support this claim. (1) The primary sources sometimes overlap, and so provide double or even triple attestation for important sayings and narratives.[4] (2) The study of Mark reveals earlier group-forms which, apparently, the Evangelist has reproduced with little change,[5] thus enabling us to use some of the advantages of Ur-Markus hypotheses without

---

[1] *Jesus Master and Lord*, 93.

[2] *La Naissance du Christianisme* (1933, Eng. Tr. by L. P. Jacks); *Les Origines du Nouveau Testament* (1936, Eng. Tr. by L. P. Jacks).

[3] *Jesus* (1935, Eng. Tr. by S. H. Hooke).

[4] Cf. T. W. Manson, *The Sayings of Jesus*, 78, 84, 109f., 123, 131, 138, 145, 216, 323–7.

[5] I have treated this point and most of the others mentioned in this summary in *The Gospel according to St. Mark*.

their embarrassments. (3) The early existence of a primitive and continuous Passion Narrative is widely acknowledged by Form Critics and others. (4) The increasing degree with which the Gospel sources are held to contain material derived from Aramaic originals carries their tradition to a point much higher up the stream. (5) The Fourth Gospel, along with the interpretative element in it, supplies independent tradition of great value to the historian. (6) The various influences apologetic, catechetical, liturgical, and doctrinal, which in various ways have modified the original tradition, can be observed and appraised, with results which show that they have by no means always obscured its meaning, but in important respects have elucidated and interpreted its significance.

For these reasons, it may be claimed, within their limitations, the Gospels, while always subject to literary and historical criticism, are a reliable guide to the study of the mind and purpose of Jesus and to the turning points of his ministry in Galilee and Jerusalem. They do not tell us all we should wish to know, and many problems remain unsolved, but we are not left in darkness with no resort but to consider how the primitive Christian communities interpreted his person and mission. In the Gospels Jesus himself can be seen and the outlines of his ministry can be traced, provided we have courage, imagination, and insight to read the primitive records aright.

Two questions of current interest, in their bearing upon the Gospel tradition, remain to be considered. The first is Typology and the second the suggestion that the Markan outline is liturgical in origin.

The fascinating theme of Typology has been treated by Dr. Austin Farrer in his book, *A Study in St. Mark*

(1952), and in a subsequent essay entitled 'Loaves and Thousands' in the *Journal of Theological Studies* (NS, iv. 1–14).

The presence of prefigurings in Biblical revelation is undoubted; they can be seen in the teaching of Jesus, the Pauline Epistles, the Epistle to the Hebrews, the Gospels, and the Apocalypse. Jesus saw deep significance in Old Testament Messianic ideas, in the teaching of Dan. vii. 13 and in the 'stone-passages' of Psa. cxviii. 22f. and Dan. ii. 34ff. He claimed that he came, not to destroy but to fulfil the Law and the prophets (Mt. v. 17), and he based belief in the resurrection on the fact that God is 'the God of Abraham, of Isaac, and of Jacob' (Mk. xii. 26f.). His choice of the Twelve points back to the twelve tribes of Israel (Lk. xxii. 30), and his action in breaking bread in the wilderness reflects the Old Testament story of the manna and the references to the Messianic feast in Isa. xxv. 6 and other passages.

In St. Paul's Epistles the sense of prefigurings is also manifest, although here the application of the principle is less creative and sometimes artificial. We recall his teaching concerning Hagar and his observation, 'which things are an allegory' (Gal. iv. 24), his insistence that the promise was made to Abraham 'and his seed' (Gal. iii. 16), his reference to the stone which followed the Israelites in their wanderings, with the interpretation 'And the rock was Christ' (I Cor. x. 4), his allusions to Jacob, Esau, and Pharaoh in Rom. ix, and, above all, his illustrative use of Old Testament narratives in I Cor. x. 1–11, culminating in the statement, 'Now these things happened unto them by way of example; and they were written for our instruction, upon whom the ends of the ages have come'. In Hebrews an impressive argument is based on the Law as 'a shadow of the good things to come'

(x. 1), and deep significance is found in the furnishing of the Tabernacle and Old Testament teaching concerning sacrifice. In Matthew the frequent use of the words, 'that it might be fulfilled which was spoken by the prophet', is characteristic, and in the Markan tradition it is not difficult to see that the first Christians had Old Testament narratives in mind in relating the stories of the Storm on the Lake (iv. 35–41), the Feeding of the Five Thousand (vi. 30–44), the Transfiguration (ix. 2–8), and the account of the Passion (xv. 29). There is a present and a forward look in the narratives of the Mission of the Twelve, particularly in Mt. x, in the account of the Apostolic Council in Ac. xv, in many Johannine stories and sayings, and in the visions of the Apocalypse.

These prefigurings are of much theological importance, provided exegesis avoids the perils of exaggeration and of fancifulness. It is, however, another matter when the Gospel of Mark is described as the symbolic structure of a numerically minded author. Dr. Farrer maintains that the Evangelist begins with the dominical symbol, 'Twelve apostles for the twelve tribes', and makes it a framework by adding two equivalent twelves, 'Twelve loaves for twelve thousands' and 'Twelve healings of particular persons' corresponding to the calling of the disciples.[1] The correspondence is interesting, but one

---

[1] We are reminded that four disciples are called in consecutive pairs (Mk. i. 16–20) and four persons are healed in consecutive pairs (Mk. i. 21–31, i. 40–ii. 12), that when Levi is called (Mk. ii. 14) a fifth healing follows (iii. 1–6), and that after the appointment of the Twelve seven more healings are recorded. The embarrassment of an additional healing is met by the submission that the Syrophoenician woman's daughter was a Gentile, exorcisms are included among the healings, and summary accounts (Mk. i. 32–4, iii. 10–12, vi. 6) are disregarded, presumably as not being numerically significant. Other numbers in Mark, the 2000 daemons of v. 13, the 200 denarii mentioned in vi. 37, the groups of hundreds and fifties (vi. 40), the two fishes (vi. 38), and the 300 denarii for which the

must doubt if it is intended and used as a framework by Mark, and still more obscure is the numerical significance of the loaves.   More serious is the objection that, contrary to the intentions of typologists, the resolution of the Gospel into cycles and paracycles must compromise its historical value.   The claim that Mark was numerically minded must minister to the view that symbolism was a guiding factor in the compilation of the Gospel, and that, in consequence, the order of events and the contents of narratives in it are matters of secondary importance. Typology, I believe, has this tendency, as the *Life of Jesus*[1] written over a century ago by D. F. Strauss abundantly shows.[2]

The second topic of current interest is the attempt of Archbishop Carrington in *The Primitive Christian Calendar: A Study in the Making of the Marcan Gospel* (1952) to show that Mark was compiled in conformity with a very early Christian lectionary based upon the Hebrew calendar.   'The Gospel', he claims, 'consists of a series of lections for use in the Christian ecclesia on the successive Sundays of the year, and of a longer continuous lection which was used on the annual solemnity of the Pascha (Passover) at which the Passion was commemorated'.[3] This theory is based on the alleged 'triadic structure' of

alabaster box of ointment might have been sold (xiv. 5), suggest still fruitful fields for typologists to till.

[1] Eng. Tr. Geo. Eliot (1848, 5th ed. 1906).

[2] With reference to the Mission of the Seventy (Lk. x. 1–20) and the number seventy, Strauss writes: 'Had Jesus, then, under the pressing circumstances that mark his public career, nothing more important to do than to cast about for significant numbers, and to surround himself with inner and outer circles of disciples, regulated by these mystic measures? or rather, is not this constant preference for sacred numbers, this assiduous development of an idea to which the number of the apostles furnished the suggestion, wholly in the spirit of primitive Christian legend?', *op. cit.*, 332f.

[3] P. xi.

the Gospel, the connexion of its outstanding narratives with Jewish feasts, and the support afforded by the chapter-divisions in Codex Vaticanus and other manuscripts. A connexion is suggested between the Seed parables of Mk. iv, the Feeding of the Five Thousand, and the Confession of Peter followed by the Transfiguration. Each, it is claimed, is connected with withdrawal to a mountain and each has to do with a mystery. 'The mystery announced in parables shortly after the First Mountain was enacted in a sacramental act at the Second Mountain, and "openly" declared shortly before the Third Mountain. It was the death and resurrection of the Son of Man'.[1] There are three mountains, three seed parables, and three announcements of the Passion. The events before the Passion cover the Hebrew year: the Preaching of John is connected with the End of Tabernacles, the Seed parables with the Spring Sowing, the Feeding of the Five Thousand with the Passover, the Feeding of the Four Thousand with Pentecost, the Transfiguration with Midsummer, and the Entry into Jerusalem and the Cleansing of the Temple with Tabernacles.

The interest of this hypothesis is manifest, and it cannot justly be objected that much in it is conjectural. It is probable also that a liturgical interest is to be seen in the Gospels, especially as regards the Last Supper, although I do not think that it goes deep or has corrupted the tradition. Goguel, who has considered the relation between the cultus and the Gospel tradition, rightly points out that to assign a dominant influence to the cultus is to try to explain something which is imperfectly known by something which is absolutely unknown, since we know nothing at all about the form of Christian

[1] P. xii.

worship in use at the time when the Gospels were composed.[1] 'It was the story which created the cultus', he observes, 'and not vice versa'.[2]   As T. W. Manson has pointed out,[3] the question arises whether the sequence of events in Mark is governed by the exigencies of the liturgical year or vice versa.   So far as the Cleansing of the Temple is concerned Manson himself has independently argued that it falls at the time of Tabernacles,[4] and he says, 'If that is so, it would suggest that the early Christian year was anchored at several fixed points, and that these were actual dated events in the ministry'.[5]

In several respects, however, misgivings arise.   Dr. R. P. Casey maintains that it is extremely unlikely that Gentile converts were won to a special devotion to the Jewish calendar, and further that there is no reason to believe that the chapter-divisions of the manuscripts are earlier than the second part of the third century.[6]   Again, the arguments for dating the ministry of John the Baptist, the Feeding of the Four Thousand, and the Transfiguration are slender indeed, if not altogether non-existent.   Finally, it is to be noted that, while Dr. Carrington affirms that 'Historicity was the essential quality of the evangelistic message; but not historicity or historical methods as we conceive them', the value of the Markan outline is likely to be depreciated if the Gospel has been built on the ground plan of a lectionary. How radical may be the results of a liturgical explanation of Gospel origins can be seen in Bertram's *Die Leidens-geschichte Jesu und der Christuskult* (1922), in which the

---

[1] *The Life of Jesus*, 165.                [2] *Op. cit.*, 188.
[3] *The Journal of Theological Studies*, NS, iv. 78.
[4] *Bulletin of the John Rylands Library*, vol. 33, no. 2, March 1951.
[5] *The Journal of Theological Studies*, NS, iv. 78.
[6] *Theology*, lv, no. 388, 362–70.

historical element is at a discount and the Gospels are described as cult-books. It is not suggested for a moment that Dr. Carrington's book is comparable with that of Bertram, but only that Bertram's discussion illustrates the radical possibilities of a full blown liturgical interpretation. Every one must agree with Dr. Manson's opinion that there is room for a good deal of further investigation, that the task will prove long and difficult, and that the Archbishop's book, like his earlier volume, *The Primitive Christian Catechism* (1940), will be a stimulus to further study.

The fact which emerges from the modern study of the Gospel tradition is its trustworthiness, provided we do not make impossible demands upon it. Bultmann's claim that we must purge it of its mythical trappings and present its teaching in terms of current existentialism[1] rests upon a radical estimate of its contents which is not justified by the most fearless inquiry. The demand that the Gospel must be 'demythologized' is sound so far as it asks us to express ancient ideas of daemons and spirits and the fantasies of apocalyptic thought in terms intelligible to the modern man, but not if we are to proceed to the task with the assumption that the tradition consists of myths of apocalyptic and Gnostic origin. A problem of special difficulty is the historical interpretation of the nature miracles. This question will arise in the story which follows. Here it is enough to say that in its modern form, the issue is not rationalism and orthodoxy, but centres in two different Christologies strongly aligned with those of the ancient schools of Antioch and Alexandria. The question for debate is not whether miracles are possible and may be regarded as forms of divine

[1] Cf. Bultmann, in *Kerygma and Myth* (Eng. Tr. by R. H. Fuller, 1953); and Ian Henderson's discussion in *Myth in the New Testament*.

revelation, but how far the narratives have been affected
by tendencies within the tradition, and, above all, by the
limitations which inevitably belong to the incarnation of
the Son of God.

## V

# THE JESUS OF HISTORY AND
# THE CHRIST OF FAITH

FINALLY, consideration must be given to the question how far the Jesus of history may be related to the Christ of faith.

On this question two observations may be made. First, Schweitzer's *Quest of the Historical Jesus* reveals how impossible it is to separate the two. When, with the best intentions, this is attempted, we obtain a more or less consistent picture of the great Galilean prophet and herald of the Kingdom of God by cutting away from the records all that appears to reflect later Christian beliefs. A strange nemesis, however, follows this method. These historical reconstructions depict a person who could never have occupied the place in history which Jesus undoubtedly fills; and the suspicion is raised that they fail because they have not come to terms with the realities of the Christ of faith. We are immeasurably indebted to the Life-of-Jesus-School, and ought never to decry its value, but must recognise that the path it blazed is labelled, 'No Through Thoroughfare'. Secondly, much the same warning applies to the road followed in the so-called Ecclesiastical Lives of Jesus, which are inspired by the desire to depict the earthly life of Jesus in close harmony with the great Christian Creeds. In these Lives a divine being is pictured who wears his humanity like a mask. The several sources are treated as if they were approximately of the same value, so that all that is needed is to piece the narratives and sayings together like the parts of a jigsaw puzzle and to fill in the gaps by bold suppositions.

The two types of portraiture are the Scylla and Charybdis of criticism, and whether it is possible to escape the perils of each can only be proved by trial. The wise course is not to attempt to find a middle path, but to keep the historical and theological aspects of the person of Christ before the mind continually, especially if we believe that Jesus cherished his own ideas concerning his person and mission. We cannot see the Jesus of history if we close our eyes to the Christ of faith; we do not see the Christ of faith except in the light of the Jesus of history. It is right, therefore, to consider, not only what inferences can be drawn from the records, but to what extent they cohere, or do not cohere, with the religious and theological aspects of his person. This is a difficult enterprise, always exposed to the dangers of perversion, but not to be neglected save at the cost of truth.

The justification in a historical inquiry for keeping in mind the Christ of faith is that it is this Christ whose story the Gospels tell, but with limitations which belong to ancient records. Even a good portrait cannot indicate the actions, intonations, and flashes of personality in a historical person, not to speak of his significance in history. If it is too much to ask for anything like this from the Gospels, we can at least look for signs and purposes of Jesus which they do not mention or suggest but faintly. Doubtless, it is perilous 'to read between the lines', but we have no discharge from this endeavour, provided we know what we are doing and are not content with arbitrary clues. If we restrict ourselves to the records, sceptical of suggestions prompted by belief, we shall not even see Jesus as he was. Many an account of his life and ministry, offered with the strictest scientific intentions, is only a charcoal sketch comparable to the first rude Christian drawings on the walls of the cata-combs of Rome. With all their faults, the Ecclesiastical Lives were written because their authors felt it necessary to remember who Christ was, even if they turned a blind eye to elements in the tradition incapable of defence. We must avoid their mistakes, but not their insight. We have to try to tell the story of one who confined himself to the limitations of human flesh, and yet has proved to be the inspiration of the ecstasy of the saints and the Lord of men of every tribe and tongue. If the dangers of dis-tortion are great, so are those of understatement. The only way to deal with bias is to know that it is there, and to ask what is its justification.

In what I have written I have assumed that the Christ of faith is not a delusion. On this matter I would say that, on any interpretation, the investigator has still to take this concept into account. Religious results which began with Jesus cannot be ignored, not even by the sceptic. The believer, however, has no choice. He has no right to pose as the impartial spectator sensitive to the charge of thinking under the sound of Church bells. He must hear the bells and be loyal to truth.

Emil Brunner has said that he who asks for proofs has not understood the nature of the Christian faith. 'It is possible', he writes, 'to mistake Christ for some other human being', and he adds, 'This alone makes it possible for us to *believe* in Him'.[1] There is warmth and appeal in these words, but I doubt if we are justified in making the venture of faith unless there are facts in the tradition which encourage us to make it. Faith is not a blind leap. Its validity is attested by a cloud of witnesses in the history of the Catholic Church, her saints, prophets, doctors,

[1] *The Mediator*, 337.

D

and martyrs, and by the stability and life of the Church herself. Even this, however, is not proof. Faith always remains a venture even to the gates of heaven. Yet it is the venture by which we see, and without which we remain blind, for the coming of Christ sifts men and judges them, so that, in the words of the Fourth Gospel, 'they which see not may see, and they which see may become blind' (ix. 39). Like the two going to Emmaus we meet Christ as One unknown, and only as he sits at meat with us are our eyes opened. Even then he vanishes out of our sight, for the final blessing which he gives is 'Blessed are they that have not seen, and yet have believed' (Jn. xx. 29).

# VI

## THE METHOD ADOPTED

IN the account of the ministry of Jesus which follows I
shall use the Markan outline as a framework, recognising that it is a sketch with many gaps, and in connexion with it I shall use material from all the Gospel
sources. I have given reasons elsewhere for believing
that the claim of K. L. Schmidt, that we have no chronological sketch of the story of Jesus, but only single stories
which are put into a framework, does not preclude us
from using Mark in the way suggested.[1] The Markan
outline is much less continuous than was formerly
supposed, especially by those who frowned upon everything which could not be brought within its bounds;
but it gives, I believe, a convincing summary of the outstanding events in the life of Jesus.[2] Its deficiencies in
respect of the Jerusalem ministry can to a large extent be
supplied from the other Gospels, including that of John,
and its relative want of sayings, parables, and discourses
can be made good from the sources Q, M, and L.

In an account such as I am attempting to give selection
from the available material is inevitable, for it is quite
impossible to place every saying and narrative in its
original context. One ought, I think, to avoid as far as
possible the expedient commonly adopted in the past
of saying 'It must have been at this time that so and so

---

[1] *The Gospel according to St. Mark*, 145–8.
[2] Cf. F. C. Burkitt, *JTS*, xxxvi. 187f.; W. F. Howard, *LQR*, July,
1927, 79; C. H. Dodd, *ET*, xlii. 400; C. S. C. Williams, McNeile's
*Introduction to the New Testament* (2nd ed.), 55–8.

happened or was said', although on occasion, when good
reasons can be given, there is justice in this practice.   It
will sometimes be necessary to discuss in separate sections
questions which affect our understanding of the course
of the ministry of Jesus, and sometimes to assemble
topical material, as Mark does, which illustrates the
leading ideas in his teaching.   This procedure is
especially necessary as regards such themes as the Kingdom of God, the Son of Man, and Messianic Suffering.
In these sections the aim is not to give a full scale treatment of the theme in question, but to indicate its bearings
on the course of events.   When incidents, sayings, and
parables are not mentioned, it is not because they are
deemed unimportant, but because those selected for
comment sufficiently illustrate the particular points
under discussion.

*PART ONE*

# THE PERIOD BEFORE THE GALILEAN MINISTRY

# VII

# THE BIRTH AND CHILDHOOD OF JESUS

ACCORDING to early Christian tradition Jesus was born in Bethlehem of Judaea in the closing years of the reign of Herod the Great (Mt. ii. 1, Lk. ii. 1–7). Our inability to speak with greater precision is due to the unsolved problems connected with Luke's account of the census under Augustus, the manner in which it is said to have been undertaken, and the date when Quirinius was governor of Syria.[1] In spite of the brilliant advocacy of Sir William M. Ramsay[2] it cannot be said that these difficulties have been successfully

---

[1] Cf. J. M. Creed, *The Gospel according to St. Luke*, 28–32. The difficulties are: (1) Josephus, *Ant.* xvii. 13. 5, says that Quirinius was governor in A.D. 6; (2) A census while Herod the Great lived (died 4 B.C.) seems unlikely; (3) A Roman census was based on residence. B. S. Easton, *St. Luke*, 20, meets the first difficulty by reading, with Tertullian, 'Sentius Saturninus' (governor 9–6 B.C.), but without manuscript support. Ramsay held that Quirinius was virtually governor 11/10–8/7 on the evidence of inscriptions at Antioch in Pisidia, but it is uncertain whether his office (one of the *duumviri* in the war against the Homonadenses) could be described as 'governor'. The reading of the *lapis Tiburtinus* (*legatus iterum Syriae*) is questioned (cf. A. J. Grieve, Supplement to Peake's *Commentary*, 19). Support would be forthcoming if the fourteen-year cycle for the census, attested by the papyri in Egypt (*VGT*, 59f.) in A.D. 20 and 34, could be shown to have obtained in Syria. The second and third objections are strong, but not insuperable, but the phrase 'their domestic hearths' in the rescript of Gaius Vibius Maximus (cf. Deissmann, *LAE*, 270f.) probably refers to places of residence. It cannot be said that the difficulties have been met, but the vindication of Luke as regards Lysanias (Lk. iii. 1) warns us against precipitancy in charging the Evangelist with error.

[2] In *Was Christ born at Bethlehem?* (1898), *Luke the Physician* (1908), *The Bearing of Recent Discovery on the Trustworthiness of the New Testament* (1915).

overcome. It may be doubted, however, if they are as important as is often supposed. If we possessed only the Gospel of Mark, like the first readers we should suppose that Jesus was born at Nazareth (cf. Mk. i. 9, vi. 1), and if our only Gospel were that of John, we should not know where he was born, although at the time when this Gospel was written the Bethlehem-tradition must have been well known. For reasons given in the Introduction it does not seem right to make the exquisite Birth Stories of Luke and the apologetic narratives of Matthew bear the weight of these historical inquiries, for which indeed they are not suited, and we have no other sources of information. The real value of the Lukan stories is the manner in which the Evangelist depicts the piety of the circles in which Jesus was born. In particular, the story of his visit to Jerusalem at the age of twelve admirably reflects the spirit of his boyhood. His questions, 'How is it that you sought me?', 'Did you not know that I must be in my Father's House?', tell us more of his intimate communion with his Father than the most ambitious reconstruction of his childhood could convey.

We shall begin our story at the point when Joseph and Mary returned to Galilee. To them subsequently were born four other sons, James, Joses, Judas, and Simon, and daughters whose number and names are not known (Mk. vi. 3). Nazareth is not mentioned in the Old Testament, nor by the historian Josephus, nor in the Jewish Talmud. In itself a town of no importance, its situation among the hills of Galilee gave it a character well suited to the boyhood of Jesus. There he grew in wisdom and in years, and in favour with God and men (Lk. ii. 52). It has often been observed that from the hills above the town he could command a view of the historic plain of Esdraelon, associated with great events in the history of Israel, and in his day crossed by caravan routes traversed by merchants and soldiers. There, undoubtedly, he gained that familiarity with nature, with birds and trees and flowers, which afterwards enriched his sayings and parables. But the incomparable gift of Nazareth was home life under the humble roof of Joseph and Mary. In that home, as the eldest member of a family, he came to know the meaning of comradeship and responsibility, especially if, as seems probable, Joseph died at an early age. Working as a carpenter, making ploughs and yokes, he knew what life meant in its toils, its joys, its strain and conflict. Little time can have been left for study, although doubtless he was taught by his parents the history and traditions of his people, and at the school of the local synagogue read and valued the Law and the Prophets. From his teaching we know that he enjoyed a close communion with his Father in prayer and meditation, and even in his early years he must have thought long and earnestly about his people and the mission he was called to fulfil.

With his dreams and hopes there may have been little sympathy in the home at Nazareth, for later, in the early days of his ministry, his family went out to apprehend him in view of the popular opinion that he was beside himself (Mk. iii. 20f.). Either then or later he addressed his disciples, and said, 'Here are my mother and my brothers! Whoever does the will of God is my brother, and sister, and mother' (Mk. iii. 34f.). Upwards of thirty years were spent in the little Galilean town, until tidings of the astounding ministry of John the Baptist led him south to the river Jordan in Judaea.

# VIII

# JOHN THE BAPTIST

IN John, the son of Zacharias, who preached and baptised in the Jordan, men heard again the long-silent voice of prophecy. By his clothing and his manner of life John showed himself to be in the succession of the prophet Elijah, but most of all by his uncompromising message. The Day of the Lord, of which the prophets had spoken, he declared was at hand. 'You brood of vipers!', he said to his hearers, 'Who warned you to flee from the wrath to come?' (Lk. iii. 7). Let them bear fruits that befit righteousness, he counselled, and not say, 'We have Abraham for our father', for of the very stones God was able to raise up children to Abraham. The note of urgency is particularly marked in John's message. The axe, he declared, was already laid at the root of the trees, and every tree not bringing forth good fruit would be cut down and thrown into the fire (Lk. iii. 9). The multitudes were bidden to share their food and clothing, the taxgatherers to collect no more than their dues, the soldiers to accuse no one falsely and to be content with their rations (Lk. iii. 10–14). In the hour of crisis the Messiah would come. In confident tones John announced the coming of one mightier than himself, the latchet of whose shoes he was not worthy to unloose, and whose coming would be one of judgement. 'His winnowing fan', he announced, 'is in his hand, thoroughly to cleanse his threshing floor, and to gather the wheat into his barn; but the chaff he will burn with unquenchable fire' (Lk. iii. 17). It is clear that John did not describe

the Messiah according to popular expectation as a national
deliverer, but as the eschatological prophet and judge.
In the sequel it will be seen how differently Jesus conceived the Messianic office.

John's stern message was the basis of an appeal to men
to repent, to face right round, and to signalise their
repentance by submitting to the rite of baptism.    Such
teaching invoked an astonishing response.    Crowds
streamed from Galilee and Judaea to hear the messenger
of the End Time, and, confessing their sins, many were
baptised by him in the waters of the Jordan (Mk. i. 4f.).
Men were conscious of the birth-pangs of a new age.

Of the greatness of John there can be no question.  At
a later time Jesus said concerning him to the multitudes:

'What did you go out into the wilderness to behold?   A reed shaken
by the wind?   What then did you go out to see?   A man clothed in
soft raiment?   Behold, those who are gorgeously clothed and live
in luxury are in kings' courts.   What then did you go out to see?
A prophet?   Yes, I tell you, and more than a prophet.   This is he
of whom it is written,

> "Behold, I send my messenger before thy face,
> Who shall prepare thy way before thee".

I tell you, among those born of women none is greater than John;
yet he who is least in the kingdom of God is greater than he'
(Lk. vii. 24–28).

In these words Jesus indicates, not only the greatness of
John, but also the fundamental contrast between the
Baptist's message of doom, and his own conception of the
kingdom as the glad news of the grace of God.

John's action in using the rite of baptism is fully in
agreement with the importance attached by the Jews to
lustrations, but it differed from these in that, like pro-
selyte-baptism, it was administered once for all.   It was a
symbol, and yet more than a symbol, if, like the Old

Testament prophets, John believed that symbolic actions
were effective.   How far he shared these beliefs we do not
know, but the positive notes in his preaching show that
in his view the essential condition in securing eschatological salvation was a radical and complete change of mind
towards God.

# IX

# THE BAPTISM OF JESUS

THE fact that Jesus was baptised by John is one of the most certain facts of the earliest tradition. Later tradition explained that John hesitated to baptise him (Mt. iii. 14f.), and the Fourth Gospel alludes to his baptism without describing it (Jn. i. 32f.). From these facts we infer that the Christians of the second and third generations found the story an embarrassment. Why had Jesus accepted John's baptism and what did his action signify? The Gospel of Mark gives no answer to this question. It regards the incident as a foreshadowing of Christian baptism: 'I baptise you with water; but he will baptise you with the Holy Spirit' (Mk. i. 8). Having regard to the nature of John's message, we may infer that what John actually said was that, whereas his baptism was a water-baptism, the Messiah would baptise men 'with fire' (cf. Mt. iii. 11, Lk. iii. 16), perhaps 'with wind and fire'. The fact is that none of our sources answers the question, and accordingly we are compelled to fall back upon conjecture. With certainty we can say that for Jesus his baptism was not 'a baptism of repentance for the remission of sins' (Mk. i. 4) so far as his personal life was concerned, for neither on this occasion nor any other does he betray any consciousness of personal sin. It may be that his action was one of self-dedication. He turned from the quiet life which hitherto had been his and dedicated himself to a mission which it was given to him to fulfil. But this explanation is not completely satisfactory. It is probable that there was a deeper motive. Not infrequently, in reading the sayings of Jesus we receive the impression that, like psalmists and prophets before him, there was a marked communal element in his consciousness. In coming to his baptism was Jesus conscious of a sense of oneness with sinful and unworthy men? Did he identify himself with his people? Did he share with them the burden of Israel's sins and, in view of the inbreaking of the New Age, perceive the need for national confession and amendment? It is difficult to answer these questions, and perhaps they cannot be answered. Nevertheless, of all the interpretations which have been proposed there is most to be said for this view.[1] If so, the Matthaean saying, 'Let it be so now; for thus it is fitting for us to fulfil all righteousness' (iii. 15), is not without relevance.

The Markan narrative tells of an experience of Jesus himself. The rending of the heavens and the voice of God were seen and heard by him alone. How far the experiences were visual and auditory we do not know, but that Jesus received the inner assurance that he was God's Son and Servant is clear. 'Thou art my beloved Son; with thee I am well pleased'. The words are significant, for they combine the Messianic language of Psa. ii. 7 and the Servant conception of Isa. xlii. 2. It is often said that at his baptism Jesus gained the conviction that he was the Messiah, but this is probably too narrow an interpretation of his experience. At the confession of Peter (Mk. viii. 29–31), and again in answer to the question of Caiaphas (Mk. xiv. 61f.), he tacitly accepted the title 'the Christ'; but it was a name with which he was never happy because of the nationalism which endeared it to the people. He thought of himself as God's Son and used this name (Mk. xiii. 32, Lk. x. 22) together with the title 'Son of Man' (Mk. viii. 31, x. 45,

[1] Cf. J. W. Bowman, *The Intention of Jesus*, 23–43.

&c.). The essence of his baptismal experience is the authentication of his filial consciousness. 'Thou my Son, the Beloved'. The conviction was permanent. Jesus was conscious of being the Son of God in a unique sense.

Jesus came to John's baptism alone and unnoticed. In contrast with the later Evangelists[1] Mark gives no indication that John pointed to him as the coming Messiah, and it is probable that it was only later and with manifest perplexity that he began to think of him as such. This view gives the best interpretation of the incident when John sent two of his disciples to Jesus with the question 'Are you he that cometh, or look we for another?' (Lk. vii. 19), and it harmonises best with the reply given to him: 'Go your way, and tell John what things you have seen and heard; the blind receive their sight, the lame walk, the lepers are cleansed, and the deaf hear, the dead are raised up, the poor have good tidings preached to them' (Lk. vii. 22). Jesus was plainly referring to his healing ministry with a pointed allusion to Isa. lxi. 1 and xxxv. 5f., but there is no need to give a literal interpretation to all the items mentioned. That he recognises the doubts and hesitations of John is suggested by his words, 'Blessed is he, whosoever shall find no occasion of stumbling in me' (Lk. vii. 23). The strong contrast between Jesus and the eschatological prophet of doom expected by John makes it difficult to decide whether the Baptist ever recognised that his ominous dream was shattered by the mercy of a greater gift from God.

[1] *V. supra.*

# X

## THE TEMPTATION

THE experience of Jesus at the Jordan led inevitably to a season of conflict and trial. Mark suggests this when he says that straightway the Spirit drove him out into the wilderness (i. 12). There, in the wild uncultivated country, he was 'tempted of Satan' (i. 13). In symbolic language, he was with the wild beasts and the angels ministered unto him. As modern men we should like to believe that Jesus did not accept popular beliefs in the existence of a personal head of the kingdom of evil, but sayings like Mk. iii. 27, which speaks of the binding of 'the strong man', and Lk. x. 18, which alludes to the fall of Satan from heaven, suggest the contrary. Manifestly, in the conditions of his earthly life, Jesus shared Biblical beliefs in the reality of daemonic powers, a conviction which is held by many Christian thinkers down to the present day. More important, however, is the nature of the experience of trial to which he was subjected.

The temptations are described in picturesque language and there is much to be said for the opinion of Albertz[1] that the artist is probably Jesus himself. Usually the temptations are described as three different experiences: the temptation to prove his Sonship by a work of power, to reveal it by a miraculous dramatic sign, and to endorse current ideas of Messiahship which involved the use of force. This view may be correct; but it is also possible that the traditional explanation interprets the threefold

[1] *Die synoptische Streitgespräche* (1921), 48.

form of the narrative too literally, and that only one possible
course of action was involved—the temptation to lead
Israel to fulfil her divine destiny even at the cost of armed
conflict with Rome. The objection that the possibility of
secondary methods can never have presented itself to the
mind of Jesus fails to do justice to the reality of his
humanity, and is therefore a form of disguised docetism.
It falls far short of the realism of the author of the Epistle
to the Hebrews who declares that Jesus our high priest
'in every respect has been tempted as we are, yet without
sin' (iv. 15, cf. ii. 18). The objection also ignores the fact
that temptation presents itself to the mind, not as evil, but
as good. Only by spiritual illumination is it seen for
what it is. Jesus rejected the temptation, saying,

> 'Begone, Satan! for it is written,
> You shall worship the Lord your God,
> And him only shall you serve' (Mt. iv. 10).[1]

We are justified in thinking that temptation tested the
quality of his Sonship and raised the implications of his
task as the Servant of the Lord. His use of the Old
Testament is significant; it shows how deeply he had
reflected upon its teaching and regarded its spiritual
meaning as authoritative. This fact appears in all the
stages of the story. The temptation to command stones
to become bread is rebutted by the citation, 'Man shall
not live by bread alone, but by every word that proceeds
out of the mouth of God' (Mt. iv. 4),[2] and the idea of
casting himself down from the pinnacle of the temple by
the words, 'You shall not tempt the Lord your God'
(Mt. iv. 7).[3] Subsequent conflicts with the scribes show
how different in spirit and understanding his use of the
Old Testament was from current Rabbinic exegesis, but

[1] Deut. vi. 13.  [2] Deut. viii. 3.  [3] Deut. vi. 16.

E

there can be no doubt that he regarded its teaching as containing the word of God.

The victory was decisive; but Luke shows insight when he says that the devil 'departed from him until an opportune time' (iv. 13). Echoes of inner conflict persist throughout the story of Jesus, not only here in the temptation in the wilderness, but also during the withdrawal to the borders of Tyre (Mk. vii. 24) and perhaps also in the retirement to Peraea (Jn. x. 40). They can be heard in the undertones of the saying, 'I have a baptism to be baptised with; and how am I constrained until it is accomplished' (Lk. xii. 50), and most of all in the prayer of Gethsemane, 'Abba, Father, all things are possible to thee; remove this cup from me; yet not what I will, but what thou wilt' (Mk. xiv. 36). Victory through conflict is the pathway of the Son of Man.

# XI

# THE INTERVAL BEFORE
# THE GALILEAN MINISTRY

FROM the Synoptic Gospels we learn nothing of what happened between the Temptation and the opening of the Galilean ministry of Jesus, but the Fourth Gospel describes a preliminary Judaean ministry (Jn. i. 19–43, ii. 13–iii. 36) during which he met some of the disciples of John, including Andrew and an unnamed disciple (i. 40), and added these, together with Simon the brother of Andrew, Philip, and Nathanael, to his immediate followers (i. 41–51). Later, after a brief return to Galilee (i. 43–ii. 12), the Evangelist records that he visited Jerusalem at the time of the Passover (ii. 13), cleansed the temple (ii. 14–22), wrought miracles which he describes as 'signs' (ii. 23–5), held an interview with Nicodemus, a ruler of the Jews who came to him by night (iii. 1–21), and continued for a time a ministry parallel to that of John in Judaea (iii. 22–30). The details of this historical construction do not invite confidence, since the Evangelist is manifestly guided by apologetic and doctrinal interests, especially as regards the relationships between the Baptist and Jesus and the significance of the cleansing of the temple, an event which probably belongs to the close of the ministry (cf. Mk. xi. 15–19). But there is more to be said for the general probability of a preliminary Judaean ministry in itself and the Evangelist may have used a tradition to this effect.

It has been conjectured that for a time Jesus worked in conjunction with the Baptist, but that after a dispute about purifying they separated and carried on their ministries independently. We should have greater confidence in this conjecture if the original text of Jn. iii. 25 were more certain. Here the Westcott and Hort text, followed by the RV and the RSV, reads 'There arose therefore a questioning on the part of John's disciples with a Jew about purifying'. Important textual authorities read 'with the Jews', but this reading seems secondary. But the singular, 'with a Jew', reads strangely, and has invited the conjecture that the original reading was 'with Jesus' or 'with the disciples of Jesus'.[1] Such a reading would give excellent sense[2] and, if accepted, would account for the rise of textual variants, but as it is without textual support, it cannot be estimated as more than a possibility. In any case the context indicates tension between the disciples of Jesus and of John (cf. Jn. iii. 26), a situation which the Evangelist uses to put into the lips of the Baptist the noble words which culminate in the confession, 'He must increase, but I must decrease' (Jn. iii. 30).

It is not certain whether Jesus taught publicly during this period or did more than converse with individuals, but there is reason to think that he met and drew to himself some who afterwards became his disciples, as John records (i. 35–51); for, on this supposition, the ready response of the four disciples in Galilee to become 'fishers of men' (Mk. i. 16–20) becomes more intelligible. The time seems to have been one of preparation for a wider and more active ministry. From Mk. i. 14 we should infer that the interval was broken by the tidings that the Baptist had been arrested and cast into prison. The

---

[1] Cf. Bauer, *Das Johannesevangelium*, 59, who prefers the usual reading; Loisy, *Le quatrième évangile*. See Hoskyns, *The Fourth Gospel*, 248.

[2] Cf. G. H. C. Macgregor, *The Gospel of John*, 90; also M. Goguel, *The Life of Jesus*, 274, who traces the conjecture to Bentley and Semler.

Gospels do not discuss, after the manner of a biography, the effect which external events had upon the actions of Jesus; but the pointed manner in which Mark says that it was 'after John was delivered up' that Jesus 'came into Galilee, preaching the good news about God', and the statement of the Fourth Evangelist during the earlier period that 'John had not yet been cast into prison' (Jn. iii. 24) prompt the inference that the arrest was decisive. The time had come to proclaim a nobler message than that of John concerning the Kingdom of God. Mark's choice of the verb rendered 'delivered up' is characteristic of his theology; it describes an action which is not merely man's doing, but is within the counsels of God.[1] Whether Jesus looked upon John's arrest in this way we do not know; if he did share this conviction, we can understand the timing of his public ministry. It was for him the will of God whatever this involved, even if he should be 'delivered up' also.

[1] Cf. ix. 31, x. 33, xiv. 41f., xv. 1, 10, 15, also Isa. xxxiv. 2, liii. 12 (LXX).

PART TWO
THE GALILEAN MINISTRY

# XII

## THE POLITICAL, SOCIAL, RELIGIOUS, AND ECONOMIC BACKGROUND

BEFORE considering the Galilean ministry of Jesus, it is necessary to glance at the external conditions of the period, since they form the background against which it must be set and interpreted.

From 4 B.C. Galilee and Peraea had been ruled over by the tetrarch Herod Antipas, 'that fox' as Jesus called him (Lk. xiii. 32), and the trans-Jordanic regions of Trachonitis, Gaulanitis, Batanea, and Panias by Herod Philip, who has been described as 'the best of the Herods'. Both were the sons of Herod the Great: they ruled, not as independent monarchs, but as suzerains of the Roman Empire, and they displayed marked Graeco-Roman sympathies which found expression in the love of architecture, in the founding and naming of Tiberias by Antipas and of Bethsaida Julias and Caesarea Philippi by Philip. The eldest son of Herod the Great, Archelaus, ruled Judaea until A.D. 6, but was deposed in that year after bitter complaints from his subjects to the Emperor Augustus, and was replaced by successive Roman procurators who governed the land under the direction of the imperial *legatus pro praetore* of Syria. From A.D. 26–36 the procurator was Pontius Pilatus, a man of cruel and rapacious tendencies, swayed by political expediency and vacillating in character.

The principal sects among the Jews were the Pharisees and the Sadducees. The Pharisees, or 'separatists', were the spiritual descendants of the Ḥasidim, the 'pious

ones', who had successfully resisted the Hellenising
policy of Antiochus Epiphanes (175–165 B.C.).   Many
of them were also scribes, or teachers of the Law, re-
nowned for their zeal for the Torah and the oral traditions
of their fathers, and reverenced as the religious *élite* of the
nation.   Entirely different in spirit were the Sadducees,
belonging mainly to the high priestly families of Jerusalem, who adhered to the teaching of the Pentateuch,
rejected later teaching concerning angels, spirits, and the
resurrection from the dead, and were anxious above all
things to maintain the political status quo, and so to avoid
conflict with the imperial power.   Akin to the Pharisees,
but much more extreme in their nationalistic sympathies,
were those subsequently known as the Zealots, to whose
excesses the horrors of the siege of Jerusalem in A.D.
68–70 were largely due.   The mass of the people, 'the
people of the land' as the Pharisees contemptuously called
them (cf. Jn. vii. 49), sat loosely to the demands of the
Law, but, none the less, honoured the Pharisees and
despised the tax collectors who gathered the imperial dues
under superiors, *publicani*, to whom the taxes were farmed.
No allusion is made in the Gospels to the Essenes, a sect
of religious purists.   Clothed in white, they lived in
lonely places, engaged in frequent lustrations, rejected
animal sacrifices, and turned their faces in worship
towards the rising sun.   To the Essenes, it has been
suggested, John the Baptist belonged, but there is no
evidence for this view.   Nor do we find Jesus at any time
in contact with them.   His early spiritual associations
are to be found rather among the 'quiet ones' described by
Luke in the Birth Stories, people who gave themselves to
worship and prayer and looked for the coming of God's
salvation (cf. Lk. i. 6, ii. 25, 37).   Last may be mentioned
the Ḥaberim ('associates'), who were not a sect and are

not named in the Gospels. Their members were Pharisees
who scrupulously observed the Law and met together
frequently for religious meals which had a quasi-sacra-
mental character.

In the Gospels we see Jesus in constant contact with the
scribes and Pharisees, but above all with the people of the
land, with outcasts, sinners, and tax-gatherers. His
allusions to the destruction of Jerusalem and its temple
show that he was alive to the perils of the political situation
and that he warned his hearers against them (cf. Mk. xiii.
1f., 14, Lk. xiii. 34f., xxi. 20–4). A Zealot, Simon the
Cananaean (Mk. iii. 18), found a place among the Twelve.
The relationships of Jesus with the Pharisees were not
always hostile (cf. Mk. xii. 34, Lk. vii. 36, xi. 37), but
for the most part he lived and worked among ordinary
people who 'heard him gladly' (Mk. xii. 37) and constantly thronged to hear him (Mk. i. 33, 45, ii. 2, 13, iii.
7–12, iv. 1, &c.). For the most part poor, and engaged
mainly in agriculture and fishing, they accorded him a
ready hearing in the towns and villages of Galilee and by
the lake of Gennesaret. They were arrested by his
prophetic declaration that the Kingdom of God was at
hand, by the freshness and originality of his teaching, and
by the magnetism of his personality. Listening to him
in the synagogues and the open air, they were attracted
by his 'words of grace' (Lk. iv. 22) and by the note of
'authority' in his teaching (Mk. i. 22).

# XIII

## THE OPENING OF THE GALILEAN MINISTRY

THE 'good news from God' which Jesus preached at the opening of his ministry is described by Mark in well-known words: 'The time is fulfilled, and the kingdom of God is at hand:[1] Repent and believe the good news' (i. 15).

From these words it appears that Jesus was in full accord with the Biblical view that in His divine activity God has an 'appointed time' (cf. Ezek. vii. 12, Dan. xii. 4, Zeph. i. 12, &c.). This 'time', he declared, was now, and in consequence the Kingdom of God was near. With the Baptist he taught that men needed to repent, that is, not only to change their minds, but deliberately to turn to God with a view to moral amendment. With him he shared the conviction that a time of crisis was at hand, but he differed from John in believing that the new era was one of grace rather than of doom. That is why he urged men to believe the good news he proclaimed.

Mark's account of the message of Jesus is very summarily stated. It is unlikely that Jesus did no more than announce the coming of the Kingdom of God and the need for repentance. He must have taught what the Kingdom was and what it implied, and it is highly probable that many of his parables, which are scattered in various contexts in the Gospels, were narrated during this period.

[1] For the rendering 'has come' cf. C. H. Dodd, *The Parables of the Kingdom*, 44–51. Cf. also M. Black, *ET*, lxiii. 289f.; E. Percy, *Die Botschaft* Jesu, 177f., who prefers the rendering 'at hand'.

Mark brings into the closest contact with the message of the Kingdom the calling of the first disciples. As Jesus passed by the lake of Galilee he summoned Peter and Andrew to follow him. As it has often been observed, the story is told from the standpoint of the disciples themselves, who were fishermen. 'Come after me', Jesus said, 'and I will make you to become fishers of men'. Going a little farther, he then called James and John, the sons of Zebedee. Without hesitation they all left their nets, and James and John their father with the hired servants, and went after him (Mk. i. 16–20). Even when we allow for the possibility of an earlier meeting in Judaea, the dramatic character of the response is striking. For them it was an unforgettable memory that Jesus had called them by the lake and that they had left all and followed him. We can only infer the motives which led them to act so decisively. Doubtless they were impressed by the personality of Jesus himself, but it is probable also that they had caught the new note in his preaching and looked for the Kingdom he had so definitely announced.

XIV

# THE MESSAGE OF
# THE KINGDOM OF GOD

WHAT was this message of the Kingdom which
Jesus proclaimed? A complete answer to this
question would entail a full study of his
teaching and its Old Testament antecedents such as
cannot be attempted in these pages. But without some
knowledge of this teaching the work and ministry of
Jesus remain an enigma. Some consideration, therefore,
of the nature of the Kingdom of God must be given at
this point.

The word 'kingdom' in the phrase 'the Kingdom of
God' is misleading, because it suggests as the primary
conception the idea of a realm or order of society established by God. Recent discussion has tended to show that
this is not the basic conception. The Kingdom of God is
not primarily, as Ritschl taught, 'the organisation of
humanity through action inspired by love',[1] although
undoubtedly such a statement well describes the conditions of human society when the Kingdom is brought into
being. The foundation idea is expressed by the Hebrew
word *malkuth*, the active *rule* of God.[2] God's sovereignty
in the hearts and lives of men expressed in the doing of
His will describes in its fundamental aspects what Jesus
meant by the Kingdom of God. The Kingdom is God's

---

[1] *Justification and Reconciliation*, 12.
[2] Cf. Dalman, *The Words of Jesus*, 96ff., G. F. Moore, *Judaism*, i.
401, T. W. Manson, *The Teaching of Jesus*, 136, Flew, *The Idea of
Perfection*, 9.

kingship, His kingly rule. This kingship, of course, implies a community, a *domain*[1] in which God's rule is fulfilled, and full justice will be given to this fact later, but we wholly miss the key to the teaching and parables of Jesus unless we realise that his primary emphasis was upon God's kingship.

A second point of vital importance concerns the time of the manifestation of God's rule. Is it present or future?

Schweitzer's *Quest of the Historical Jesus* has familiarised us with the term 'consistent eschatology' and the idea that the Kingdom is wholly future, a view which is everywhere implied in the writings of Bultmann.[2] Equally familiar is the phrase 'realised eschatology' used by C. H. Dodd in his *Parables of the Kingdom*[3] and elsewhere, a term which summarises the idea that the Kingdom is actually present in the person and work of Jesus, especially in his exorcisms and works of healing. In these questions it is wise not to allow ourselves to adopt an attitude of 'Either-Or', *Entweder-Oder*, since we can do so only by ignoring or explaining away sayings and parables which do not support the alternative chosen. The teaching of Jesus is eschatological throughout, but this view does not prevent us from believing that he taught that the Kingdom was present in himself and his ministry, but was also future in the sense that it was to be consummated by God.

Among sayings in which the emphasis is future may be mentioned the prayer, 'Thy kingdom come' (Lk. xi. 2 = Mt. vi. 10), the saying about the patriarchs coming from the east and west and sitting down in the Kingdom of

[1] Cf. Flew, *Jesus and His Church*, 35.
[2] *Die Geschichte der synoptischen Tradition*, 113–38, *Jesus and the Word*, 35–45, *Theology of the New Testament*, 3–11.
[3] *Op. cit.*, 34–80. Cf. also J. Jeremias, *Die Gleichnisse Jesu*, 96, 162; E. Percy, *Die Botschaft Jesu*, 175–224.

God (Lk. xiii. 29 = Mt. viii. 11), the prophecy that bystanders would not taste death until they saw the kingdom come with power (Mk. ix. 1), and, above all, the declaration of Jesus at the Last Supper, 'Truly, I say to you, I shall not drink again of the fruit of the vine until that day when I drink it new in the kingdom of God' (Mk. xiv. 25). On the other side, the sayings which imply that the Kingdom is already present in Jesus and his deeds include: the saying concerning casting out devils by the finger of God (Lk. xi. 20, Mt. xii. 28, 'by the Spirit of God'), the message to John the Baptist (Lk. vii. 22f. = Mt. xi. 5f.), the declaration, 'Blessed are the eyes which see what you see' (Lk. x. 23f. = Mt. xiii. 16f.), the words about the Kingdom exercising its power[1] (cf. Lk. xvi. 16 = Mt. xi. 12f.), the statement, 'The kingdom of God is within you' (Lk. xvii. 20f.), and the parables of the Seed growing secretly (Mk. iv. 26–9), the Mustard Seed (Mk. iv. 30–2 and Lk. xiii. 18f. = Mt. xiii. 31), the Leaven (Lk. xiii. 20f. = Mt. xiii. 33), the Hidden Treasure (Mt. xiii. 44), and the Pearl (Mt. xiii. 45f.).

If we could place all these sayings and parables in their original context, we should have invaluable evidence concerning the course of the teaching of Jesus, but in most cases this is quite impossible. Neither can we assume that one series is earlier than the other. All that we can say is that probably many of the sayings which imply that the Kingdom is present are naturally associated with the opening of the Galilean ministry and its later stages. The opening statement in Mk. i. 15, whether we translate it, 'The kingdom of God has come', or 'is at hand', shows

---

[1] Cf. Otto, *The Kingdom of God and the Son of Man*, 108–12, T. W. Manson, *The Sayings of Jesus*, 133–5, E. Percy, *Die Botschaft Jesu*, 191–7.

this, and the same inference is prompted by the reply of
Jesus, when charged with collusion with Beelzebul
(Lk. xi. 20), his message to the Baptist (Lk. vii. 22f.),
and the parables already mentioned.

The people of Galilee must have been startled and
impressed by a new note in the teaching of Jesus, the
declaration that the Rule of God was near and even present
already in his deeds and the idea that Satan was bound
(Lk. xi. 22, cf. Mk. iii. 27). Only so can we explain why
his hearers cried, 'What is this? a new teaching with
authority!' (Mk. i. 27) and why the report concerning
him went out far and wide throughout all the surrounding
region of Galilee (Mk. i. 28). Especially must they have
been struck by the contrast between the message of Jesus
and that of John the Baptist. Whereas the Baptist
announced the coming of the Kingdom as a prophet of
doom, Jesus spoke of it as the good gift of God, as the
most precious thing which a man might possess and into
the sharing of which he might enter. John's metaphors
were those of a threshing floor, a winnowing fan, and an
axe laid at the root of the tree, but Jesus pictured the joy
of finding buried treasure and of lighting upon a precious
pearl. The Kingdom, as Jesus presented it, had the
explosive force of leaven and all the potency of growth
found in a tiny mustard seed. It was not a social pro-
gramme which men might carry out for themselves, but
the work of God already in progress. A man might sow
his seed, but the blade, the ear, and the full corn followed
in a way beyond his knowledge, his task being to put in
his sickle because the harvest was come (Mk. iv. 26-9).

We cannot fail to see that great hopes and keen expectancy were encouraged by the earliest preaching of
Jesus, hopes in which he himself shared. He taught and
believed that he and his hearers were living in days of

F

fulfilment.   Then or later he said to his disciples concerning signs of the rule of God: 'Blessed are the eyes
which see what you see!   For I tell you that many
prophets and kings desired to see what you see, and did not
see it, and to hear what you hear, and did not hear it'
(Lk. x. 23f.).   Great things had happened and were about
to happen!   'Something greater than Solomon is here',
'something greater than Jonah'!   These are the notes
we hear in all the accounts of the Galilean ministry.   The
rule of God was near, even at the doors!

# XV

## THE KINGDOM OF GOD AND
## THE ELECT COMMUNITY

I N the account we have given of the Kingdom of God
we have seen that there is an element wanting, the
idea of a community or domain in which the rule of
God is exercised. Is this want supplied by the concept
of the Son of Man?

It is the merit of Otto's *Kingdom of God and the Son of
Man* that the two ideas are brought together, in the sense
that Christ himself is the Elect of God, the one destined
to be the Son of Man. He is the Eschatological Re-
deemer conscious of a ministry which is essential to the
fulfilment of the rule of God. This is a true and moving
thought, but it is manifest that there would be a still
closer connexion between the two concepts if the Son of
Man is not only Jesus himself but the Elect Community
of which he is the Head; in short, if the 'Son of Man' is
both a *communal* and a *personal* name. This communal
interpretation was advanced by T. W. Manson in his
*Teaching of Jesus* (1931) and is strongly supported by
C. J. Cadoux in *The Historic Mission of Jesus*[1] and by other
writers,[2] but it is still a hypothesis open to discussion and
is perhaps not capable of demonstration.[3] Although this
book is not primarily concerned with critical discussions, it will be of advantage to the reader to summarize
the arguments on which the collective interpretation

---

[1] Pp. 90–103.     [2] Cf. M. Black, *ET*, lx, 33f.
[3] It is rejected by E. Percy, *Die Botschaft Jesu*, (1953), 239n, as
*unnatürlich und gezwungen*, but without discussion.

rests, inasmuch as, if it is accepted, it is of importance in the account of the life and ministry of Jesus here presented.

First, the 'one like unto a son of man' described in Dan. vii. 13, from which Jesus drew the idea of the Son of Man, is a symbolic figure which represents 'the saints of the Most High' to whom a kingdom is given by God, 'the Ancient of Days' (Dan. vii. 18, 21f., 27).[1] Thus, from its beginnings, the concept is communal. Secondly, the collective interpretation is in harmony with the use of the pronoun 'I' in the Psalms, where it often describes the people of Israel; and it is in line with the representation of the Servant of the Lord which in Deutero-Isaiah oscillates between the portrait of a community and an individual.[2] Thirdly, both the Kingdom of God and the Son of Man are concepts eschatological in origin and range; each appears to imply the other, since there is no rule of God apart from those over whom it is exercised and no elect community save where God reigns. Fourthly, some of the Son of Man sayings, including Mk. viii. 38, Lk. xii. 8f. = Mt. x. 32, also Mt. x. 23, Lk. xii. 40, xvii. 22, 24, 26f., 30, and perhaps Lk. xvii. 25 and Mk. viii. 31, are susceptible of a communal interpretation, and such parables as the Fig Tree in Summer (Mk. xiii. 28f.), the Thief at Night (Lk. xii. 39 = Mt. xxiv. 42f.), and the Waiting Servants (Lk. xii. 35-8, Mt. xxiv. 42, cf. Mk. xiii. 33-7) can be similarly applied. Fifthly, Son of Man sayings relating to the Parousia are in most cases connected by Luke with the Galilean ministry and its later stages (cf. Lk. xii. 8f., 40, xvii. 22-30, xviii. 8b), by Matthew also in x. 23, xix. 28a, and editorially in xiii.

---

[1] Some scholars (e.g. Nils Messel and T. W. Manson) think that the Son of Man in I Enoch can also be interpreted in a communal sense. Cf. Manson, *The Teaching of Jesus*, 228f.

[2] Cf. Manson, *op. cit.*, 227-30.

37–43, and by Mark in viii. 38. Otherwise Matthew includes most of these sayings and many parables in the framework provided by the Apocalyptic discourse of Mk. xiii in harmony with the current expectation of the Parousia of Christ. This arrangement, in part at least, is editorial. The distribution of the sayings suggests that many of them were uttered during the ministry itself, and not exclusively at its tragic close. But if this is so, is it probable that Jesus was speaking of his own return in glory? It seems more probable that either he distinguished the Son of Man, as a supernatural figure from himself, or that he was speaking of the Elect Community of the Son of Man; and of these alternatives the second is the more probable. Sixthly, on the assumption that many of the Son of Man sayings are early and communal, the absence from these sayings of allusions to suffering and death, while later Son of Man sayings, which predict the Passion, do not refer to the Parousia,[1] becomes intelligible. The two groups belong to different stages and circumstances in the historic ministry.

These arguments present a strong *prima facie* case for the communal interpretation of the term 'Son of Man', but, in default of sayings expressly affirming this view, the submission cannot be said to be conclusive. There is, nevertheless, sufficient evidence to encourage the inquiry whether the collective interpretation furnishes a fruitful clue for the study of the life and ministry of Jesus, and it may be claimed that the extent to which it does this is so far a confirmation of the hypothesis. The possibility cannot be ignored that the tendency in primitive Christianity to apply the Parousia sayings to the idea of the Second Coming of Christ may have obscured their earlier relevance to the Elect Community, and may thus

---

[1] Cf. Bultmann, *Theology of the New Testament*, 29.

have destroyed evidence. Ideas that were superseded or embraced in larger conceptions cannot be expected to have left pronounced traces in the Gospel tradition. It is not a conclusive objection to the collective interpretation that unambiguous testimony to this usage cannot be found.

There is, however, a further consideration which supports the attempt to use the communal view of the Son of Man in interpreting the course of the ministry of Jesus. It is important to observe that, even if the collective interpretation is rejected, and the name 'Son of Man' is regarded as exclusively a personal title of Jesus, it is still necessary to think of the Elect Community in connexion with the Kingdom of God. Sayings like those concerning the 'little flock' (Lk. xii. 32), eating and drinking in Christ's Kingdom (Lk. xxii. 30), and the gathering of the Elect from the four winds (Mk. xiii. 27), and the implications of parables like the Great Supper (Lk. xiv. 16–24), leave us no option. Moreover, as previously maintained, the kingship of God cannot be exercised *in vacuo*; it implies a community. The Kingdom of God, the downfall of Satan, the gathering of the Elect, and the New Age are an indissoluble eschatological whole, no matter whether the eschatology is futuristic, realised, or both. Now the want of a name for the domain or community has paralysed much contemporary discussion concerning the Kingdom. The collective view of the Son of Man supplies a name in the usage of Jesus, and therefore meets a need; but even if we think that usage is not established, we must still allow for 'the thing signified', in these circumstances the nameless domain of the kingly rule of God. The delusive idea that Jesus thought only of his community in the later stages of his ministry, if indeed he thought of it then, has been fostered by the

presence of the word *ecclesia* only in Mt. xvi. 18 and
xviii. 17. Moreover, as every one knows, the authenticity of these sayings has been repeatedly challenged.
In point of fact, as R. N. Flew has maintained,[1] they do
not stand in the forefront of the argument. The community, subordinate to the kingly rule of God, is implicit
in the teaching of Jesus from the beginning, from the
very moment when he proclaimed the near advent of the
Kingdom in the declaration, 'The Kingdom of God is at
hand' (Mk. i. 15). The calling of the disciples is the
beginning of the community and the ministry of Jesus
is the means by which it is brought into being. Apart,
therefore, from discussions concerning 'the Son of Man'
a communal element in his teaching is a vital clue to his
mission. If this is so, the significance of the title, important and revealing as it is, is not a decisive issue. The
thing signified, and not the name, is the primary consideration. The value of the collective interpretation
is that it names the community otherwise implied.

The communal interpretation, it has been rightly held,
does not exclude the use of the name 'Son of Man' by
Jesus in a personal sense, as the Head of the Elect Community, its Lord and Master, and it is in no way inconsistent with the fact that he speaks of the Son of Man in
terms of Messianic suffering; it does not even exclude the
idea of his return in glory. The sayings in Mk. viii. 31,
ix. 12, 31, x. 33f., 45, and xiv. 62 are not 'prophecies
after the event', but proofs that, as the Son of Man, Jesus
thought of his ministry in terms of suffering and victory.[2]
This question will be considered later at the point where
it arises in the story of Jesus.[3] It is mentioned here

---

[1] *Jesus and His Church*, 123–36.
[2] Cf. V. Taylor, *The Names of Jesus*, 31–5.
[3] See pp. 142–5.

because the full meaning of the doctrine of the Son of
Man is seen only when the life of Jesus is considered as
a whole.

In considering these matters much depends on whether
we are ready to recognise the presence of a development
in the thought of Jesus during the course of his ministry.
Many scholars are not willing to admit such a development. They prefer to think that the course of his life
work was clear to him at least from his baptism onwards,
and they find an allusion to the idea of the Suffering
Servant in Mk. i. 11, in the words of the divine voice, 'My
Son, the Beloved', although, in fact, the words reflect
Isa. xlii. 2, and not Isa. liii. Jesus, they believe, saw his
pathway clearly from the beginning. It is to be noted that
even this view does not exclude development; it merely
assigns it to the 'hidden years' before the baptism; for it
will hardly be contended that contact with life did not
shape that filial consciousness which is reflected in the
story of the visit of Jesus to the Temple at the age of
twelve (Lk. ii. 49). It is far better to recognise during the
ministry as well as in youth that 'he grew in wisdom as in
age' (Lk. ii. 52), and to take seriously the teaching of the
Epistle to the Hebrews that he 'learned obedience by the
things which he suffered' (v. 8). The sayings regarding
the Kingdom point in this direction. At the beginning of
his ministry Jesus proclaims that the Kingdom is close
at hand (Mk. i. 15) and indeed is present in a true sense
in his mighty works (Lk. xi. 20), but, as we have seen,
he still bids his disciples pray that the rule of God may
come (Mt. vi. 10). The saying, 'Truly, I tell you, there
are some standing here who will not taste death before
they see the kingdom of God come with power' (Mk. ix.
1) implies that it will appear shortly, but it leaves the impression of an expectation less immediate than Mk. i. 15.

Later still he says, with reference to the Parousia, 'Of that day or that hour no one knows, not even the angels in heaven, nor the Son, but only the Father' (Mk. xiii. 32), and at the Last Supper he speaks of drinking the fruit of the vine new in the Kingdom of God (Mk. xiv. 25). In these eschatological sayings the day is not necessarily relegated to the distant future; it may be thought of as near; but the sense of immediacy is much less pronounced and everything is left to the Father's good pleasure.

The development is organic. It is crudely conceived if it is regarded as progress through error, as if one concept is first accepted, and then rejected, and finally replaced by another. The thought of the rule of God persists all through the teaching of Jesus and it determines all his conceptions of his mission. Like the theme of a fugue it appears and reappears and continues to the end. The Kingdom and the domain are not separate and parallel conceptions. The Kingdom is basic. Such changes as historical criticism can detect concern the conditions on which the divine rule depends, the time of its consummation, and the manner and means by which it comes into being. This principle makes the life and ministry of Jesus a unity; it constitutes it a whole. The Kingdom of God is the Ariadne thread which links together the Mission of the Twelve, the Fellowship Meal in the wilderness, the withdrawal to the region of Tyre, the teaching on Messianic suffering after the great day near Caesarea Philippi, the journey to Jerusalem, and the Cross and Passion.

# XVI

# OTHER LEADING IDEAS IN
# THE TEACHING OF JESUS

JUST because the rule of God is central in the teaching of Jesus ideas closely associated with this theme repeatedly appear in his sayings and parables. It matters little that we cannot date them or place them with confidence in their original context. They belong to his teaching throughout his ministry and must have been characteristic of the Galilean mission.

Pre-eminent in this respect is the emphasis Jesus laid on the love of God. It is illustrated in the first part of the parable of the Lost Son (Lk. xv. 11–24), which is a story drawn from life to depict that love. In the allied parables of the Lost Sheep (Lk. xv. 3–7) and the Lost Coin (Lk. xv. 8–10) the words about joy in the presence of the angels of God over one sinner that repents are not meant to distinguish the angels from God, but in a characteristically Semitic manner describe the joy of God Himself in forgiveness. In the parables of the Friend at Midnight (Lk. xi. 5–8) and the Unjust Judge (Lk. xviii. 2–8) he argued *a fortiori* from the most unpromising circumstances and people to the boundless compassion of God. First among the commandments he set the *shema*, recited daily by every Jew, 'Hear, O Israel: The Lord our God, the Lord is one; and you shall love the Lord your God with all your heart, and with all your soul, and with all your mind, and with all your strength' (Deut. vi. 4, Mk. xii. 29). There was, however, no sentimentality in his teaching. God, he taught, demanded the unquestioning

obedience of men who, when they had done all that was
commanded, were to say, 'We are unworthy servants, we
have done that which it was our duty to do' (Lk. xvii.
10).

Closely connected with the teaching concerning God
was the joyous message that His love is extended to the
unworthy. This truth lies behind the parables of the
Labourers in the Vineyard (Mt. xx. 1–15) and the
Pharisee and the Taxgatherer (Lk. xviii. 9–14). In
harmony with it was the action of Jesus himself in calling
Levi at the place of toll (Mk. ii. 14), in healing Samaritan
lepers (Lk. xvii. 12–19), and in his compassion towards
the city harlot (Lk. vii. 36–50). It is one of the strands
woven into the texture of the Gospel by St. Paul when he
writes, 'But God commends his own love for us in that
while we were yet sinners Christ died for us' (Rom. v. 8).
In the words and actions of Jesus men heard a new note
in religious teaching, and while some were repelled by its
apparent levity, others found in it unexpected hope in the
possibility of divine forgiveness.

The same love and the same forgiveness, Jesus taught,
were to be extended by men to others. 'Should you not
have had mercy on your fellow servant, as I had mercy on
you?', he asked in the parable of the Two Debtors (Mt.
xviii. 23–35), and when he told how the unforgiving
debtor was handed over to the tormentors, he sternly
added, 'So also my heavenly Father will do to every one
of you, if you do not forgive your brother from your
heart'. Similarly, in the prayer which he taught his
disciples, he charged them to say, 'Forgive us our sins,
for we ourselves forgive every one that is indebted to us'
(Lk. xi. 4). They were not to judge, but to take out first
the beam from their own eye before they saw clearly to
remove the splinter from their brother's eye (Lk. vi. 42).

'Love your enemies', he said, 'and do good, and lend, despairing of no men' (Lk. vi. 35). So would they be sons of the Father in heaven who makes his sun to rise on the evil and the good, and sends rain on the just and on the unjust (Lk. vi. 35, Mt. v. 45).

These ideas are not separate and distinct from the teaching about the kingly rule of God; they unfold its meaning and bring out its implications. We shall not understand the inwardness of his teaching and the impression it created unless we see how intimately all the themes of his message were related one to another. It was the greatness of the challenge with which he confronted men which led him to bid them count the cost, and not to be like a foolish builder who, when he has laid a foundation, is not able to finish, or a rash king who does not consider whether he has forces at his command sufficient to meet those of an enemy (Lk. xiv. 28–32). 'Whoever does not bear his own cross, and come after me', he said, 'cannot be my disciple' (Lk. xiv. 27, Mt. x. 38, Mk. viii. 34).[1]

It is tempting to continue drawing upon the rich store of the sayings and parables of Jesus, but our purpose is not to attempt to give a full account of his teaching, but to indicate how it is related to his mission and ministry. The connexion is direct and unmistakable. By his words, as well as by his deeds, Jesus fulfilled his purpose in living and dying for the kingly rule of God.

---

[1] Interpreting the saying literally, Ernst Percy, *Die Botschaft Jesu*, 168–74, claims that it is no community-formation, but an authentic word of Jesus.

# XVII

## THE CHARACTER OF
## THE EARLY GALILEAN MINISTRY

CAN we picture to ourselves the character of the early Galilean ministry? Fortunately, in Mk. i. 21–39 we have a vivid description of a day in the life of Jesus which by wide consent is based on the best tradition, perhaps ultimately upon the recollections of Peter. It consists of four narratives linked together by geographical and temporal statements, in this respect standing in contrast with the section ii. 1–iii. 6, which almost immediately follows. The section does not give any account of the teaching of Jesus, and for this it will be necessary to look later at Mt. v–vii and Mk. iv, but it does describe what we may regard as a typical day in the early ministry.

In i. 21 we find ourselves in the synagogue at Capernaum, the modern *Tell Ḥûm* by the lake of Galilee. Although the subject-matter of the teaching is not given, it is clear that it made a profound impression. The people 'were astonished at his teaching: for he taught them as having authority, and not as the scribes' (i. 22). The interest is concentrated upon the outburst of a man described as one 'with an unclean spirit'. Apparently, he had an uncanny knowledge of something superhuman in the personality of Jesus, and speaking in the name of the devils by which he believed himself to be possessed, he cried out, 'Why dost thou meddle with us, thou Jesus of Nazareth? Thou art come to destroy us' (i. 24). This incident reflects the view, shared in those days by

educated and uneducated alike and held it would seem by
Jesus also, that many mental disorders were due to
daemon-possession.   Jesus treated the man on this
assumption.   'Be silent', he cried, 'and come out of him'.
The word of authority prevailed.   With a paroxysm and
loud cries the man was healed, to the amazement of all.
The teaching of Jesus, they saw, was matched by his
deeds.   'What is this?', they said.   'A new teaching with
authority!   Why!  he commands  even  the  unclean
spirits, and they obey him!'   It is not surprising that
Mark says that the report concerning him went out at
once everywhere throughout Galilee and the adjacent
region (i. 28).

Leaving the synagogue, Jesus entered the house of
Simon and Andrew, with James and John.   Simon's
wife's mother was not able to attend upon them.   Hoping
perhaps that he would heal her, they told him of her fever.
Coming to her and taking her by the hand, Jesus raised
her up, with the result that the fever left her and she
served them.   When evening came the sick and the
daemon-possessed were brought to Jesus, so that, with
hyperbole, Mark declares that 'all the city was gathered
together at the door'.   The sick were healed and many
devils were cast out.   Mark adds that a charge of secrecy
was laid upon the daemons, 'because they knew him'.

I have described these stories much as they are told
because they confront us with two problems which still
provoke debate: the healing power of Jesus, including his
exorcisms, and the injunctions to secrecy, which, according to Mark, he frequently imposed.   To-day, when
the results of psychotherapy are matters of common
knowledge, few New Testament scholars dispute the
healing powers of Jesus, but recognise that his methods
were spiritual, dependent upon his personality and his

fellowship with God in faith and prayer. Exorcism is another matter. It is difficult not to think that belief in daemon-possession belongs to a pre-scientific age, and that, in the fulness of his humanity, Jesus shared contemporary ideas. It should be added, however, that scholars of repute accept the reality of possession and claim examples of its presence among primitive peoples to-day.

The injunctions to secrecy raise an important question. In a famous discussion, *Das Messiasgeheimnis in den Evangelien* (2nd ed. 1913), Wrede explained them as a literary device on the part of Mark to explain why the Messiahship of Jesus was not recognised until after the resurrection. Many scholars have had little difficulty in rejecting the theory in this extreme form, pointing to the Confession of Peter, the Transfiguration, and the Entry into Jerusalem, to the reply of Jesus to Caiaphas (Mk. xiv. 62), the title on the cross (Mk. xv. 26), and the improbability that the first Christians would have held Jesus to be the Messiah unless he had been recognised as such *before* the resurrection. This is a strong case, but a more positive answer is needed. The injunctions to secrecy are historical, even if the idea is overworked by Mark, but they call for explanation. Only in part are they explained by the desire of Jesus to prevent futile Messianic demonstrations. The fuller explanation is the immense gap between popular views and Messiahship as Jesus understood it. For him it was not merely an office, but a redemptive ministry to which he was committed.[1] He did not deny that he was the Messiah, but he could not accept a title which, in terms of current expectation, ran counter to his conceptions of his mission.

[1] See further V. Taylor, *The Gospel according to St. Mark*, 122–4; *ET*, lix. 146–51, 'The Messianic Secret in Mark'.

This view is powerfully supported by the last story in Mk. i. 21–39. Very early on the following morning Jesus, without the knowledge of his disciples, left Capernaum and went into the wilderness for prayer. Later, in Mark's expressive phrase, Simon and his companions 'tracked him down' and greeted him with the reproachful tidings, 'All men are seeking you'. To them he gave what must have seemed a most discouraging reply, 'Let us go to the next towns, that I may preach there also; for that is why I came out' (i. 38). He was speaking, not merely of his departure from Capernaum, but of his ministry, as indeed Luke perceived in his version of the reply, 'For therefore was I sent' (Lk. iv. 43). He clearly regarded his message concerning the kingdom as of greater importance than his works of healing.

If the story of the leper (Mk. i. 40–5) belongs to this period,[1] it shows that, none the less, the appeal of suffering could not be denied. Afflicted with a distressing skin disease, not to be confused with modern leprosy, the man appears to have been confident that Jesus could make him clean. For reasons which can only be conjectured Jesus was angry.[2] Nevertheless, he stretched out his hand and touched him, with the authoritative word, 'I will; be clean'. Then, moved with deep emotion, he bade the man keep silence about the cure and show himself, in accordance with the Law, to the priest taking with him the prescribed offering. The result was that Jesus was compelled for a time to avoid towns. Yet even so, people came to him from every quarter.

---

[1] Mark introduces the story without any temporal or geographical link (contrast Mt. viii. 1 and Lk. v. 12), a noteworthy restraint which is significant when statements are made about the artificiality of his outline.

[2] Reading ὀργισθείς.

# XVIII

## CONFLICTS AND
## MISUNDERSTANDINGS

MARK records that after an interval of some days Jesus returned to Capernaum and resumed his ministry there (ii. 1f.). From this point on-wards, however, it is not possible to record his story in detail, for, as compared with i. 21–39, the section ii. 1–iii. 6 is a pre–Gospel topical compilation, which without any attempt at chronological arrangement was intended to show how Jesus came into mortal conflict with the scribes and Pharisees.[1] It records the things which caused offence: his claim to forgive sins (ii. 6–10), his association with taxgatherers and sinners (ii. 16f.), his disciples' neglect of fasting (ii. 18–20), their breach of the laws of the sabbath (ii. 22–6), and his own action in healing on the sabbath day (iii. 1–5). These incidents which happened at different times and can no longer be dated, are strung together in order to answer a question which puzzled the first Christians: 'How was it that Jesus, who went about doing good and proclaiming the advent of the kingdom of God, came in the end to a shame-ful death?'. A similar topical collection in xi. 27–xii. 37, shows how his enemies sought to entrap him on such issues as the exercise of his authority (xi. 27–33), the payment of tribute money to Caesar (xii. 13–17), and the resurrection (xii. 18–27). Some of these incidents

---

[1] This suggestion of Form Critics explains why iii. 6, the death plot of the Pharisees and Herodians, appears so early in the Gospel, as well as the use of the title 'Son of Man' in ii. 10 and 28.

may well belong to the Galilean ministry.   Although we can no longer place them in their historical context, they show how steadily the opposition of the hierarchy to Jesus grew, until in the end his destruction was inevitable.

Another topical section, Mk. iii. 19b–35, illustrates the reactions which the ministry of Jesus provoked.   Many people thought him mad and his relatives went out to restrain him (iii. 21), while the scribes attributed his works of healing to collusion with Satan (iii. 22).   The reply of Jesus to this charge illustrates his skill in controversy and reveals the ideas he held concerning himself and his ministry.   'How can Satan cast out Satan?', he asked.   'If a kingdom be divided against itself, that kingdom cannot stand.   And if a house be divided against itself, that house will not be able to stand.   And if Satan has risen up against himself, and is divided, he cannot stand, but has come to an end' (iii. 23–6).   If it was by Beelzebul, he argued, that he cast out devils, by whom did their sons cast them out?; but if by the finger of God, then indeed had the kingdom of God come upon them (Lk. xi. 19f.).   The spoiling of Satan's goods meant that Satan had been bound.   'When the strong man fully armed guards his own court, his goods are in peace; but when a stronger than he shall come upon him, and overcome him, he takes from him his armour in which he trusted, and divides his spoils' (Lk. xi. 21f.).   A parallel version of this saying is found in Mk. iii. 27, 'No one can enter a strong man's house and plunder his goods, unless he first binds the strong man; then indeed he may plunder his house'.   It may be that, in the light of his temptation, Jesus believed himself to be the binder of Satan, as many commentators have suggested,[1] but it may

---

[1] Cf. V. Taylor, *The Gospel according to St. Mark*, 241f.   J. Jeremias, *Die Gleichnisse Jesu*, 101f.

also be that he attributed the binding to God.[1]  In either case his belief shows that he regarded daemon-possession as the ravages of a beaten foe, and therefore as a sign of the imminence of the rule of God.  Jewish belief, as illustrated in Isa. xxiv. 22f. and in the Apocalyptic literature, interpreted the binding and casting down of Satan as an event connected with the last things.  The sayings quoted above, and Lk. x. 18, illustrate the 'realised eschatology' of Jesus, his belief that the events of the last time were happening now in his exorcisms.

Yet another topical section, vii. 1–23, may be mentioned because it shows how conflicts with the scribes arose on the question of ceremonial washings and the oral interpretation of the Law.  The fact that we cannot fit the stories and sayings it contains into a biographical account of the life of Christ in no way precludes its significance for the character of his ministry.  It shows how fundamental issues were inevitably brought into the foreground.  Noticing the carelessness of the disciples in respect of ceremonial washings, the scribes made it a ground of attack upon their Master.  'Why do your disciples not live according to the tradition of the elders but eat with defiled hands?' (vii. 5), they asked.  Jesus immediately took up the challenge, recalling the words of Isa. xxix. 13, 'This people honours me with their lips, but their heart is far from me'.  'Well did Isaiah prophesy of you hypocrites', he said, 'You leave the commandment of God, and hold fast the tradition of men'.  Either then or on some other occasion he reminded them of the current scribal ruling, that if a son declared on oath that the provision he might otherwise have made for his parents was *qorban*, that is, devoted to God, his oath was binding.

---

[1] So Creed, Rawlinson, and Branscomb, and recently Ernst Percy, *Die Botschaft Jesu*, 181–7.

Thus, by their tradition they had made void the word of God. In this context Mark mentions one of the most revolutionary of the sayings of Jesus: 'Hear me, all of you, and understand: there is nothing outside a man which by going into him can defile him; but the things which come out of the man are those which defile the man' (vii. 15). Mark's comment is 'Thus he declared all foods clean' (vii. 19). The comment goes beyond the immediate intention of Jesus, for had he been understood from the beginning to mean as much as this, the vision of Peter on the housetop at Joppa (Ac. x. 9–16) and the sharp dispute at Antioch on the question of eating with Gentiles (Gal. ii. 11–21) would not have been possible. Nevertheless, the Evangelist rightly caught the drift of Jesus's teaching and its ultimate implications, and saw how inevitable the final break with Judaism was.

Recent study of the parables has emphasized the fact that some of them reflect the conflicts of Jesus with the scribes and Pharisees. They were weapons by which he defended his teaching, especially his good news of the graciousness of God towards the unworthy. The parable of the Labourers in the Vineyard (Mt. xx. 1–15) is of this character. It reaches its climax in the words, 'Is your eye evil because I am good?'. 'This', says Jeremias, 'is the justification of the Gospel absolutely: so is God, so gracious'.[1] There is manifestly a polemical element in the parable of the Pharisee and the Taxgatherer (Lk. xviii. 9–14) in the contrast between the Pharisee's prayer and that of the taxgatherer, 'God be merciful to me a sinner'. In the parable of the Lost Son (Lk. xv. 11–32) the elder brother is typical of the scribes and Pharisees who

---

[1] *Die Gleichnisse Jesu*, 113; cf. C. H. Dodd, *The Parables of the Kingdom*, 122f.

frowned upon the attitude of Jesus to sinners,[1] and the parable of the Two Sons (Mt. xxi. 28–31) must be interpreted similarly in the light of the saying, 'Truly, I tell you, the taxgatherers and the harlots go into the kingdom of God before you'. Most controversial of all is the parable of the Wicked Husbandmen (Mk. xii. 1–8). C. H. Dodd points out that Mark says that the rulers recognised that it was aimed against them (xii. 12), and adds, 'and we can well believe it'.[2]

The last named parable belongs to the ministry at Jerusalem, and others mentioned above may have been uttered then or during the later Galilean ministry, but some of these parabolic thrusts may have been made much earlier, for the conflict with the scribes and Pharisees which reached its climax in Jerusalem goes back to the earliest days, to the moment, in fact, when the nature of his teaching became apparent.

---

[1] B. T. D. Smith, *The Parables of the Synoptic Gospels*, 194, questions whether the parable had a controversial purpose. But cf. Jeremias, *op. cit.*, 108, Dodd, *op. cit.*, 120. Smith thinks that the parable of the Faithful and Unfaithful Servants (Lk. xii. 42–6, Mt. xxiv. 45–51) was a warning directed to the priestly aristocracy and that of the Talents (Mt. xxv. 14–30, Lk. xix. 12–27) a warning addressed to the scribes, *op. cit.*, 158, 168. Cf. Jeremias, *op. cit.*, 126; Dodd, *op. cit.*, 151, 160.

[2] *Op. cit.*, 126. Jeremias, *op. cit.*, 59, 127.

# XIX

## THE CHOICE AND APPOINTMENT
## OF THE TWELVE

THE Galilean ministry had not long been in progress
before Jesus took the decisive step in choosing and
appointing the Twelve. The growing opposition
of the scribes and Pharisees may have had something to do
with his action, but the more important motives are
mentioned in the Markan narrative of iii. 13–19a.

Mark records that Jesus went up into the hill country
and called to himself those whom he desired (iii. 13).
Probably the hills to the north of the lake are meant.
The selection was made from those who were already his
disciples. The number 'twelve' corresponds, and apparently was meant to correspond, to the twelve tribes of
Israel (cf. Lk. xxii. 30); it indicates that Jesus intended
the chosen disciples to play a real part in his mission.
Among the reasons for the appointment Mark mentions
two: the desire of Jesus that the Twelve should be in
daily association with himself and his intention to commission them to preach and to cast out daemons (iii. 14f.).
The preaching to which they were called was the proclamation of the coming of the Kingdom, as is indicated
later in the accounts of the Mission of the Twelve.[1]
The gift of authority to cast out daemons meant that they
were leagued with Jesus in his fight against the powers of
evil (iii. 22–7). It may also have been his intention that
the Twelve should exercise functions of government in the
future Messianic community. Such a function is cer-

[1] Cf. Lk. ix. 2, x. 9, Mt. x. 7.

tainly mentioned later in Lk. xxii. 29f. after the Last Supper in the saying, 'As my Father appointed a kingdom for me, so do I appoint for you that you may eat and drink at my table in my kingdom, and sit on thrones judging the twelve tribes of Israel'.[1]

As given by Mark the names of the Twelve are Simon, James and John, the sons of Zebedee, Andrew, Philip, Bartholomew, Matthew, Thomas, James the son of Alphaeus, Thaddaeus, Simon the Cananaean, and Judas Iscariot (iii. 16–19). Several of these men are merely names to us: there is no record of any part, other than the mission of the Twelve, which they played in the life of the primitive Church. Moreover, the later lists given by Matthew (x. 2–4) and Luke (vi. 14–16, Ac. i. 13), although in substantial agreement with Mark's account, do not agree with it exactly, and we can only conjecture the identity of Thaddaeus, Lebbaeus (mentioned by some MSS. in Mt. x. 3), and Judas of James (named in the Lukan lists). More important still, outside the Gospels the Twelve are expressly mentioned in three passages only, in Ac. vi. 2, I Cor. xv. 5, and Apoc. xxi. 14 ('the twelve apostles of the Lamb'). Instead of 'the Twelve', we read in the Acts and the Epistles of 'the Apostles', a larger body which includes, not only Peter, James, and John, but also others who were not of the Twelve, including James the Lord's brother, Paul, Barnabas, Silas (I Thess. ii. 6), Andronicus and Junias (Rom. xvi. 7), and others whose names we do not know. Missionaries and witnesses of the resurrection, these men went forth to Syria, Cyprus, Antioch, Asia, Macedonia, Achaia, and

[1] The Matthaean form of the saying (xix. 28), derived from M, is inserted in the Markan narrative concerning Rewards (x. 28–31). Apparently an isolated saying in the tradition, it is eschatological in character, as also in Lk. xxii 29f., where it appears in a context which mentions the Mission of the Seventy (xxii. 35f.).

Rome, establishing new communities and laying the foundations of the infant Church. Such are the facts. What is the explanation?

To deny the historical character of the choice and appointment of the Twelve is unwarranted, so deeply is the tradition concerning them rooted in the Gospels. They appear to have been chosen for a special purpose connected with the Galilean mission fulfilled in the ministry of the Twelve when they went out two by two 'without purse, and wallet, and shoes' (Lk. xxii. 35) to proclaim the advent of the kingdom of God. Before and after this mission they are merged in the larger group of 'the disciples', from whom they are distinguished in such a phrase as 'those who were about him with the twelve' (Mk. iv. 10), and pointedly in the case of Judas Iscariot who is described as 'one of the twelve' (Mk. xiv. 10, 20, 43). The conclusion to be drawn is that the appointment of 'the Twelve' was of the things that pass, because its original purpose was fulfilled. In the expansion of Christianity the future lay with 'the Apostles'.[1]

[1] See further V. Taylor, *The Gospel according to St. Mark*, Note B, 'The Twelve and the Apostles', 619–27.

# XX

## THE GREAT SERMON

SOON after the choice of the Twelve, either upon a mountain itself or more probably on a level place below (Lk. vi. 17), Jesus gave to his disciples a manifesto or address which has come to be known as 'the Sermon on the Mount'. In the forms in which it is recorded it is clearly a compilation, but that an address was delivered is intelligible in itself and is well attested in the primitive sources. Matthew has combined two independent accounts of the Sermon, from Q and M, while Luke gives the Q version, but both Evangelists have not unnaturally included in it isolated sayings kindred in character which could not be located exactly in the story of Jesus. Impossible as it is to reconstruct the Sermon in its entirety, it is probable that it began with a number of Beatitudes, in which Jesus described the mind and spirit of those who submit themselves to the rule of God and the principles which should guide their relationships with others, followed by a group of Antitheses (Mt. v. 21–48), in which injunctions of the Law are set in contrast with new and more spiritual interpretations introduced by his majestic 'I say unto you', and by various sayings regarding judging, almsgiving, fasting, and prayer, the 'Golden Rule', the practical tests of good fruits in life, and the necessity of doing the will of God. It may also be that the teaching about anxious care, with the counsel, 'Be not therefore anxious for the morrow, for the morrow will be anxious for itself' (Mt. vi. 25–34), belongs to the Sermon, although Luke places it in another context (xii. 22–31), for it accords well with that spirit of perfect trust in God which was to be the mark of the new community.   The Sermon ends with the parable of the Two Houses, one built upon the rock and the other upon sand (Mt. vii. 24–7, Lk. vi. 47–9).   The significance of the parable turns upon the necessity of obeying the words of Jesus.   Both men hear, but one acts and the other does not, with security in the hour of testing in the one case and ruin in the other.   Whether the reference is to the final judgement or to the crises which arise in life and history it is impossible to say,[1] but the arresting point in the parable is the incomparable note of authority in the challenge of Jesus.   'Why call you me, Lord, Lord', he asked, 'and do not the things which I say?' (Lk. vi. 46).   It was with these words that he introduced the parable, which does not hesitate to poise the future of men upon the response they make to his commands.

[1] Cf. T. W. Manson, *The Sayings of Jesus*, 61f.; J. Jeremias, *Die Gleichnisse Jesu* (1952), 139f.

# XXI

## THE LAKESIDE TEACHING

ALTHOUGH the story of the lakeside teaching of Jesus cannot be told in detail, we receive a living impression of its character in the summary statement of Mk. iii. 7–12, which describes a great multitude which came to him 'from Galilee, Judaea, Jerusalem, Idumaea, beyond the Jordan, and about Tyre and Sidon'. So great was the crowd that he commanded his disciples that a little boat should be in attendance upon him as a refuge from physical pressure, for he healed many, so that those who had plagues fell upon him in their eagerness to touch him. Men with unclean spirits, when they saw him, fell down before him and greeted him as 'the Son of God', but Jesus charged them not to make him known. In this vivid passage there is a touch of hyperbole in the list of places mentioned, but it well illustrates the amazing popularity of the ministry of Jesus at this period as a teacher and healer.

One such day in particular is described in Mk. iv. 1 when recourse to the boat was necessary as Jesus told the parable of the Sower.[1]  It is possible that in his allusions to the way, the shallow ground, and the soil choked with thorns, Jesus was thinking of his own experience as a teacher; but the main emphasis of the parable lies upon the amazing harvest, thirtyfold, sixtyfold, a hundredfold, which follows the sowing of the seed in the good ground. The parable expressed his belief that, despite unresponsive

[1] Much of the material in this chapter appears to have been added by Mark for topical reasons, especially 10–13, 14–20, and 21–5.

hearers, the field was white unto harvest (Jn. iv. 35).[1] Especially notable is the emphasis he laid upon the need for attentive hearing: 'He who has ears to hear let him hear' (Mk. iv. 9). Jesus meant men not to miss the signs of the times and, in particular, the proofs of the redemptive working of God.

As is well known, similitudes, parables, and illustrative stories played a great part in the teaching of Jesus. They were used by him to elucidate his teaching, but we cannot assume that Jesus always sought to be immediately understood. The parables were used to provoke thought and encourage reflection. In part, although only in part, this fact may account for Mark's introduction of the difficult saying in iv. 11f.:

'Unto you is given the mystery of the kingdom of God: but unto them that are without, all things are done in parables: that seeing they may see, and not perceive; and hearing they may hear, and not understand; lest haply they should turn again, and it should be forgiven them'.

Many attempts have been made to soften the rigour of this saying,[2] which, as it stands, speaks of the parables as if they were intended to conceal the truth and to expose men to inexorable doom. It seems more probable, however, that misled by the ambiguity of the Hebrew *mashal*, which can mean 'riddle' as well as 'parable', and influenced by current difficulties of interpretation and his view that the person and teaching of Jesus were hidden during his ministry, Mark has introduced a genuine saying of Jesus into an alien context. The saying adapts

---

[1] Cf. C. H. Dodd, *The Parables of the Kingdom*, 180–3. So also Jeremias, *op. cit.*, 94f.

[2] See especially the attractive suggestion of T. W. Manson, *The Teaching of Jesus*, 78f., that ἵνα in iv. 12 mistranslates the Aramaic *d<sup>e</sup>*, actually used in the Targum, which ought to have been rendered οἵ, 'who'.

the well-known saying in which Isaiah describes his call from the standpoint of his actual experiences as a prophet (cf. Isa. vi. 9ff.). So Jesus may well have spoken of his ministry at a later period, perhaps at the time when he uttered his lament over the towns of Chorazin, Bethsaida, and Capernaum (Lk. x. 13–15).[1] Mark gives a truer estimate of the use of the parables at the end of the section iv. 1–34, after he has recorded the parables of the Seed growing Secretly and the Mustard Seed, in the words: 'And with many such parables he spoke the word unto them as they were able to hear it, and without a parable he did not speak unto them: but privately to his own disciples he expounded all things' (iv. 33f.). This statement recognises that sometimes parables needed to be explained, and it is in agreement with Rabbinic practice, but it stands in contrast with iv. 11f. when it is applied to parables. Possibly iv. 33f. led Mark to insert the traditional explanation of the parable of the Sower in iv. 14–20 and the saying on the lamp in the little group of sayings in iv. 21–5. When this saying was uttered it is impossible to say, but it is well placed in the chapter, since it teaches that a lamp is intended to give light and that revelation is the ultimate purpose of hiding. The emphasis on the necessity of paying attention in the saying in iv. 23, 'If any one has ears to hear, let him hear', is characteristic of Jesus, and probably not less so his

---

[1] See the excellent discussion of Jeremias, *op. cit*, 7–12, who argues that the saying is inserted by Mark in view of (1) the change of situation (cf. 10); (2) and of the hearers; (3) other additions in iv (e.g. 10–20); (4) the double answer to 10 in 11f. and 13ff.; (5) the formula καὶ ἔλεγεν αὐτοῖς in 11. 11f., he maintains is a very old logion, typically Palestinian, which, as Manson has shown, agrees with Tg. Isa.vi. 10, and, with the rendering, 'To those that are without all is full of riddles', probably belongs to the period after Peter's confession, and has therefore nothing to do with the explanation of parables. The 'mystery of the kingdom' is that of its present in-breaking in Jesus's word and work (p. 12)

injunction, 'Take heed what you hear' (iv. 24). It will be seen that, despite the editorial arrangement of the chapter, we receive a living impression of the nature of the lakeside teaching. In various ways, by parables and by pointed sayings, Jesus sought to bring home to his Galilean hearers the fact of the inbreaking of the kingdom of God.

# XXII

## MIGHTY WORKS

On the late afternoon of the day to which the account of the parabolic teaching is assigned Mark records that the disciples took Jesus, just as he was, in the boat to the other side of the lake (iv. 35f.). During the voyage one of those sudden storms for which the lake is notorious arose, as the wind swept down the narrow gorges near the east shore. In Mark's graphic account, 'the waves beat into the boat, insomuch that the boat was now filling' (iv. 37). Meantime, Jesus was asleep on the wooden headrest. In their extremity the disciples awoke him and addressed him curtly. 'Master', they cried, 'don't you care that we are perishing?'. Thus addressed, Jesus awoke, rebuked the wind, and said to the sea, 'Peace, be still'. The wind ceased and there was a great calm. 'Why are you fearful?', he asked his disciples, 'have you not yet faith?'. A great awe fell upon them, and they said one to another, 'Who then is this, that even the wind and the sea obey him?'.

The story has been told with a minimum of interpretation because it raises in an acute form the question whether Jesus wrought miracles upon nature. There does not appear to be any need to question anything that is recorded in the narrative. Even the sudden calm is true to the geographical conditions of the lake. It has been suggested that Jesus rebuked the disciples, and not the wind, but it seems unlikely that eyewitnesses could have been mistaken upon this point. That he should have rebuked the elements reflects an attitude to nature quite

different from that of the modern man, but it is in
harmony with his use of hyperbole in his saying about
the uprooting and removal of a mountain, 'Be taken up
and cast into the sea' (Mk. xi. 23). We can infer therefore that he spoke to the wind and the sea in implicit
dependence upon his Father's will. Further, the question
of the disciples is natural and can have been asked among
themselves on the spot. But did Jesus actually still the
storm?

Opinion upon this question is divided and will probably continue to be divided.[1] Nature, it is said, is not
a closed system and miracles are not impossible. On the
contrary, they are part of the Gospel itself. It may be
doubted, however, if these arguments settle the question.
In the end decision turns on the issue, whether, within
the accepted limitations of his humanity, Jesus is likely
to have wrought miracles upon nature, and whether it is
not probable in cases of this kind that the original
incidents have been given a miraculous interpretation,
not necessarily after the lapse of time, but even from the
beginning. Those who think in this way will prefer to
speak of the stilling of the storm as a miracle of divine
providence, and will be predisposed to find a miraculous
colouring in other narratives similar in character, but not
numerous, such as the Multiplication of the Loaves (Mk.
vi. 30–44), the Walking on the Water (Mk. vi. 47–52),
the Cursing of the Fig Tree (Mk. xi. 12–14, 20–22), the
reference to the swine in the Gerasene Demoniac (Mk.
v. 1–20), and perhaps also the Raising of Jairus'
Daughter (Mk. v. 21–43).

The story about the demoniac (Mk. v. 1–20) is linked
by the Evangelist to the account of the storm by the
words, 'They came to the other side of the sea, to the

---

[1] See earlier, Prolegomena, p. 33f.

country of the Gerasenes' (v. 1). Landing on the eastern
shore, at Kersa or Kursa, Jesus was met by 'a man with an
unclean spirit', or as we should say to-day, a man afflicted
with the tortures of a divided personality. The demoniac
was evidently a peril to his neighbours, for he had often
been bound with chains and fetters, and as often he had
broken them. No man had strength to tame him.
'Night and day', Mark writes, 'among the tombs and on
the mountains he was always crying out, and cutting
himself with stones' (v. 5). The details are taken from
life,[1] and equally the spirited dialogue which follows.
Apparently, when Jesus had commanded the unclean
spirit to come out, the cure was not immediate, for the
man expostulated, 'What have you to do with me, Jesus,
Son of the Most High God? I adjure you by God, tor-
ment me not'. Thereupon Jesus asked him his name, for
it was widely believed in antiquity that knowledge of a
name gave power. To his question the strange reply,
which reveals a knowledge of Roman armies, was given
'My name is Legion; for we are many'. The alternation
of the singular and the plural in the man's words here and
elsewhere is very lifelike and reveals the depth of his
malady. The one point of serious difficulty in the narrative is the destruction of the swine, and for this fact no
better explanation has been offered than the suggestion
of panic caused by the paroxysm of the man's cure.[2]

The narrative of Jairus' daughter (Mk. v. 21–43)
belongs to the subsequent return of Jesus and his disciples to Galilee. Where the incident happened we do
not know; Capernaum or Bethsaida have been suggested.

---

[1] It is unnecessary, with Dibelius, *From Tradition to Gospel*, 89, to
account for the narrative as a story concerning a Jewish exorcist erroneously
ascribed in the tradition to Jesus.

[2] Cf. J. Weiss, *Das älteste Evangelium*. 189.

H

Again the narrative is full of artless details. The little girl is at the point of death and the ruler of the synagogue beseeches Jesus to come and lay his hands on her, so that she may be made well and live (v. 23). Jesus consents and they set out for the house. At this point in the most natural manner the narrative is intercalated with that of the woman with the issue of blood (v. 25–35). 'If I touch even his garments', she said, 'I shall be made well'. Mark comments on the story, explaining that Jesus was conscious that power had gone forth from him and dramatises the narrative by ascribing to Jesus the question, 'Who touched my garments?', and by saying that 'he looked round to see her who had done this' (v. 32). 'Daughter', said Jesus, 'your faith has made you well; go in peace, and be healed of your disease'.

What happened at the house of Jairus is a question of the greatest difficulty. The later Evangelists have no doubt that the girl was restored from death (cf. Mt. ix. 18, Lk. viii. 55), in this respect interpreting their Markan source. Mark himself may have held the same view, but the astonishing thing about his narrative is that another opinion is possible. On the one hand, the messengers report that the girl is dead, the members of her family lament her death, and the witnesses in the bed chamber are lost in amazement; on the other hand, Jesus ignores the tidings of death, bids Jairus fear nothing, says to the weeping family, 'The child is not dead, but sleeps', and taking her by the hand commands, 'Little girl, I say to you, arise'. The action of recalling a living spirit from the power of death stands in a different category from those of multiplying loaves or cursing a fig tree, and we know too little about the moments preceding and following death to dogmatise upon the matter. Moreover, the verb translated 'sleeps' can be used metaphorically of the sleep of death,[1] although that is not its primary meaning. The hypothesis of resurrection is not therefore excluded. Against this opinion there is little evidence elsewhere that Jesus raised the dead,[2] and good commentators[3] have taken the view that the girl was aroused from a state of trance or coma. On the whole, this seems the best explanation of the narrative.

It is not to be supposed that the four incidents described in Mk. iv. 35–v. 43 were the only events which happened in the period covered, for, as K. L. Schmidt has pointed out, there may be a gap between verses 20 and 21. Mark wrote on the basis of a good tradition which preserved only a fragmentary knowledge of the movements of Jesus from one side of the lake to the other, and has recorded 'mighty works' which stood out in succession in the recollections of an eyewitness, presumably Peter. Other events preceded or followed the restoration of Jairus' daughter, including probably visits to towns on the lakeside or within the interior of Galilee. We need not hesitate to infer that he continued in synagogues and in the open air to speak of the Kingdom of God in sayings and parables.

---

[1] Cf. Bauer, *Wörterbuch zum NT*, 606, on the meaning of καθεύδω, normally used of natural sleep (but see I Thess. v. 10).

[2] The story of the young man at Nain (Lk. vii. 11–17) may be a case of premature burial and the historical basis of the didactic story of the raising of Lazarus (Jn. xi. 1–46) is not known.

[3] C. H. Turner, *St. Mark*, 30, suggests that, if we could read Mark's narrative without presuppositions derived from Mt. and Lk., we should naturally conclude that Jesus knew the case to be one of coma. Cf. Plummer, *St. Mark*, 152; Creed, *St. Luke*, 124; McNeile, *St. Matthew*, 126.

# XXIII

# THE END OF SYNAGOGUE PREACHING

A<small>T</small> the point we have reached in the story of Jesus Mark relates that he came into 'his own country', presumably to Nazareth, and preached in the synagogue there. Luke independently records the story (iv. 16–30) at a point much earlier in his Gospel, and Mark's local statement, 'from thence' (vi. 1), is indeterminate. We cannot therefore be sure when the incident happened, but he uses this adverbial form so rarely in narratives[1] that we have reason to agree with K. L. Schmidt[2] that he found it in his source, and by the use of the phrase 'his own country' rather than the place name Mark appears to anticipate the dramatic significance of the event.

On the sabbath day Jesus began to teach in the synagogue. Evidently his fame had preceded him. In their astonishment many of his hearers asked, 'Whence hath this man these things?', and 'What is the wisdom given to this man?' (vi. 2). They wondered also concerning the meaning of the 'mighty works' wrought by his hands. No small part of their perplexity arose because they had known him in childhood and youth, his parents, and his brothers and sisters (vi. 3, cf. Lk. iv. 22). Luke also vividly depicts the attention of the congregation; the eyes of all were fixed upon him, and all wondered at the words of grace which came from his mouth (Lk. iv. 20, 22). Without explanation Mark goes on to say that they

---

[1] Elsewhere the word appears in narratives only at vii. 24, ix. 30 and x. 1 (in sayings twice in vi. 10f.). Matthew has it in narratives 11 times.
[2] *Op. cit.*, 153.

were offended at him. So abruptly does this statement appear that conjecture alone is possible. Either accounts of different visits have been telescoped or the provocative sermon Luke describes had been preached (Lk. iv. 24–7). Jesus replied in proverbial words, 'A prophet is not without honour, save in his own country, and among his own kin, and in his own house'. Luke records that the incident ended in attempted violence (iv. 29f.) from which Jesus escaped. Mark makes the bold statement that, beyond laying his hands upon a few sick people, Jesus was able to do no mighty work there, and that he marvelled because of their unbelief (vi. 5f.).[1] This statement is perhaps the boldest comment which the Gospels contain. It reveals the reality of the humanity of Jesus, the supreme emphasis which he laid upon faith, and the tide of criticism and hostility to which he was exposed, despite the enthusiastic interest of the crowds. Nowhere again is he said to have taught in a synagogue. That phase of his public activity was over. As Mark records 'he went round about the villages teaching' (vi. 6b). We may surmise that there he received a more ready response to his message than in the larger towns and in more pronounced religious circles.

It is at this point in his ministry that he launched the mission of the Twelve, an event closely bound up with his conception of his work and destined, I believe, to exercise a decisive influence upon its character.

---

[1] Luke has no parallel to this statement. Matthew modifies it in the more sober and discreet form, 'And he did not many mighty works there because of their unbelief' (xiii. 58), one of the many signs that he has edited his Markan source. Cf. also Mt. viii. 25 and Mk. iv. 38, and Mt. xix. 17 with Mk. x. 18.

# XXIV

## THE MISSION OF THE TWELVE

AT some time subsequent to the rejection at Nazareth Jesus sent forth the Twelve, two by two, to announce the imminent coming of the Kingdom of God. Like Jesus himself, they were to go to 'the lost sheep of the house of Israel' (Mt. x. 6) with the message 'The kingdom of God is come nigh unto you' (Mt. x. 7, Lk. ix. 2, x. 9), to summon men to repent, to cast out devils, and to heal the sick. The importance of this event in the primitive tradition is shown by the fact that versions of the charge given to the disciples are found in every one of our four main Gospel sources, in Mark, in Q, in M, and in L.[1] Moreover, the instructions themselves reveal its climacteric character. The equipment of the Twelve was to be reduced to the barest essentials. They were to take with them no bread, no begging-bag, and not a copper in their girdles. According to Mark they were allowed a staff and sandals, but in Q even the staff and shoes are prohibited and only a single under tunic is allowed (Mt. x. 10). Contrary to the immemorial custom of the east, like Gehazi[2] of old they were to salute no man in the way. They were to accept the first hospitality that was offered; to pay no attention to the kind of food provided; to bespeak peace on the house that received them; to shake off the dust under their feet against the place that would not hear them. The time

---

[1] See Mk. vi. 8–11. For Q see Lk. x. 2f., 8–12, 13–16 (with parallels in Mt.); for M Mt. x. 5–8, 9–16, 23–5, 40–xi. 1; for L Lk. x. 1, 4–7, 17–20. So T. W. Manson, *The Sayings of Jesus*, 73–6, 179–84, 256–9.

[2] Kings iv. 29.

was one of harvest, but the labourers were few, and they were to pray the Lord of the harvest that He would send forth labourers into His harvest (Mt. ix. 37f.). They were the representatives of Jesus, *sheluḥim*, men sent, so that to receive them was to receive him, and to receive Jesus was to receive him that sent him (Mt. x. 40).

Everything in the records goes to show that the Twelve were sent out under an overwhelming sense of urgency. A crisis was imminent; it was the eve of expected events. Nothing could be more mistaken than to think of their mission as a simple evangelistic tour, in which, so to speak, they were 'tried out' as healers and preachers. The instructions show that they were to be 'like an invading army, and live on the country'.[1] They were heralds of the swift advent of the Kingdom of God.

The general rejection of the 'thoroughgoing eschatology' of Schweitzer has tended to obscure the emphasis he rightly laid upon the crucial importance of the mission and its decisive importance for Jesus himself.[2] Schweitzer was fully justified in insisting that 'the whole history of "Christianity" down to the present day . . . is based on the delay of the Parousia'.[3] He was mistaken in supposing that Jesus looked for the end of history in the coming of a supernatural Son of Man from heaven, but not in the view that for him the inbreaking of the Kingdom was near. What Jesus expected, and what he sent forth the Twelve to announce, was the speedy coming of the rule of God

[1] Manson, *op. cit.*, 181.

[2] 'The thoroughgoing eschatological school makes better work of it (the withdrawal of Jesus from public work and his resolve to die). They recognise in the non-occurrence of the Parousia promised in Mt. x. 23 the "historic fact", in the estimation of Jesus, which in some way determined the alteration of his plans, and his attitude towards the multitude', *The Quest of the Historical Jesus*, 358.

[3] *Op. cit.*, 358.

and the setting up of the Messianic community of the Son of Man. It was in this expectation, I think, that he assured the Twelve that they would not have gone through the cities of Israel before the Son of Man would be come (Mt. x. 23).

In recent exposition the genuineness of Mt. x. 23 has been widely disputed on the ground that it appears in a section of Matthew which is a compilation and in which the interest is centred on the early Christian mission to the Gentiles. It is said to be the Judaistic Christian explanation of the prohibition in Mt. x. 5f., 'Go not into the way of the Gentiles, and enter not into any city of the Samaritans'.[1] As Streeter puts it, 'It is not that Gentiles cannot or ought not to be saved, but the time will not be long enough to preach to all, and Israel has the first right to hear'.[2] 'It reflects', says Manson, 'the experience and the expectations of the primitive Palestinian Church'.[3] This explanation may well be a correct account of the meaning of Mt. x. 23 in its present context and as Matthew uses it, but only, I suggest, if it already existed in the tradition as a genuine saying of Jesus. In Mt. x. 5–23 it is exploited, but not invented, for who would have invented a prophecy of Jesus which was not fulfilled? It is probable therefore that criticism will need to look again at a saying which may have an important bearing on the mission of the Twelve.

Another saying, which throws light upon the mind of Jesus at this period[4] is given by Luke in his account of the return of the Seventy (x. 17–20). When the disciples

---

[1] Cf. B. T. D. Smith, *The Gospel according to St. Matthew*, 123.

[2] *The Four Gospels*, 255.

[3] *The Sayings of Jesus*, 182.

[4] The saying is relevant whether we regard the Mission of the Seventy as a doublet of the Mission of the Twelve or whether we interpret them as successive events.

returned, exulting that even the daemons were subject
unto them in his name, Jesus replied, 'I was beholding
Satan fall as lightning from heaven' (x. 18). The downfall of Satan in the last days was a current Jewish Christian
eschatological expectation, as we see from Apoc. xii. 9,
where in the oracle it is said that Satan 'was cast down to
the earth, and his angels with him'. In Lk. x. 18 Jesus
plainly has this idea in mind and speaks of it in terms of
'realised eschatology'. But what is the tone of the saying,
and how does it bear upon the mission? In his *Die
Gleichnisse Jesu*, 101n, Jeremias mentions the Dutch
scholar, M. van Rhijn, who explains the saying as ironical.
Jesus sees that his disciples are in danger of overestimating
their success in the matter of exorcisms, and wishes to say
that not so quickly will Satan be overcome. Jeremias
himself thinks that the saying does not suggest irony.
Does it, however, suggest disappointment? Is the
meaning that Jesus had looked to see[1] Satan fall from
Heaven, in whatever sense we may interpret the figure,
but alas! in vain? Certainly there is reproof in his
address to the disciples, 'Rejoice not that the spirits are
subject to you; but rejoice that your names are written in
heaven' (x. 20), but it is difficult to be sure about the tone
of a recorded saying. In any case Lk. x. 18–20 is significant. The passage contains two eschatological concepts,
the allusion to the fall of Satan and a reference to the Book
of Life; it suggests that the Mission was no ordinary missionary tour, but an event of crisis connected with the Kingdom of God and with the community of the Son of Man.

It may be objected that we are reading more into the
incident than the Gospels relate. This objection is valid;

---

[1] In this case the imperfect ἐθεώρουν is conative. Unfortunately,
whether an imperfect is conative or not depends on the context. Cf. Ac.
vii. 26 and xxvi. 11.

but there is every justification for going beyond the bare records. All the sources give extracts from the charge to the Twelve, but the narrative passages, Mk. vi. 7, 12f., Mt. x. 1, 5, Lk. ix. 1f., 6, x. 1, 17, are of the scantiest and most general character. It is manifest that at the time the Gospels were written, the significance of the mission had long been forgotten. It is from this cause, it may be added, that the place of the Twelve themselves in the earliest tradition is so obscure.[1] The justification for reading more into the incident is the disparity between the narrative passages and the extraordinary character of the injunctions laid upon the disciples. It was not for simple evangelistic activity that they were charged to ignore the traditional salutations of the east, to travel surprisingly light, to receive without comment the barest sustenance, to hurry on from place to place, to reject even the dust of unreceptive towns, always announcing the imminence of the Kingdom of God. They are not preachers, but delegates; not teachers, but heralds; and their hearers are tested by their response, by whether they receive their message and repent. The mission presents the challenge of an impending event. For this reason it is entirely unique in the annals of evangelic activity. The task of the Preaching Friars and of the leaders of the Evangelical Revival offers only a faint analogy. For a closer parallel we have to think rather of the despatch of a fiery cross among the Highland clans, except that the message is not a call to arms but a summons to hear. It is this fact, hidden but visible behind the tradition like the lower writing in a palimpsest, which justifies the belief that the mission and its sequel are fundamental to the understanding of the story of Jesus.

No small part of the significance of the mission is that it

---

[1] See earlier, p. 92.

failed.  In the words of Schweitzer, but with a different
interpretation of the title 'Son of Man', 'the disciples
returned to him; and the appearing of the Son of Man
had not taken place'.[1]  But the failure was immensely
fruitful.  In this respect the record is an epitome of the
earthly life of Jesus, which is the story of victory through
defeat, of rejection followed by exaltation.  Jesus was not
mistaken, and never was mistaken, in believing that the
Kingdom of God was at hand, for it is always at hand, even
to-day.  Had the expectation of the coming of the Kingdom been an error, it would have been renounced;  but
Jesus did not renounce, and never withdrew, his conviction that the rule of God was near, as the subsequent
sacramental meal in the wilderness and his solemn reply
to the challenge of Caiaphas so clearly show.  The disappointment was one of clock-time.  Expectation had been
foreshortened.  The consummation looked for had not
happened.  Nevertheless, it lives on in the story of Jesus,
and from now onwards it appears in grander but crimson
colours.  Through the failure of the mission, the fate of
John the Baptist, and his own profound meditation upon
the Servant teaching of Isa. liii, Jesus was led to seek a
deeper interpretation of the doctrine of the Son of Man.  It
is to the birth and elucidation of the conviction that 'the
Son of Man must suffer' that we must trace his withdrawal
from public teaching, and apparently for a time from his
daily association with the Twelve, during the period when
he retired to the borders of Tyre (Mk. vii. 24), thence to
emerge in renewed contact with his disciples in the villages
of Caesarea Philippi, when he asked of them, 'Who do men
say that I am?', and more pointedly, 'Who do *you* say that
I am?' (Mk. viii. 27-9), and finally to go to Jerusalem to
suffering, death, resurrection, and victory.

[1] *Op. cit.*, 357.

# XXV

# AFTER THE MISSION OF THE TWELVE

THE immediate sequel to the mission of the Twelve is one of the most difficult problems in the story of Jesus. There is a gap in the Markan outline at this point, which Mark fills with the story of Herod's fears (vi. 14–16) and an account of the murder of John the Baptist (vi. 17–29). All that he expressly relates with reference to the mission is that the apostles returned to Jesus and told what they had done and taught (vi. 30). Forthwith the story of the departure into a wilderness place follows, and incidents, including the Feeding of the Five Thousand, are recounted.

Important sayings, however, imply that other events, not mentioned by Mark, took place, probably at this time, for they express a sense of disappointment which does not harmonise with the joy and expectancy with which the Twelve were sent forth. The saying, 'To what shall I liken the men of this generation?', is of this character. 'They are like children sitting in the market place,' Jesus said, 'and calling to one another, We piped to you, and you did not dance; we wailed, and you did not weep' (Lk. vii. 31f. = Mt. xi. 16f.). These words do not belong to the first days of the Galilean ministry, as their sad tone and the contrast Jesus proceeds to draw between the Baptist and himself indicate: 'John the Baptist has come, not eating bread, nor drinking wine, and you say, He has a daemon. The Son of Man has come, eating and drinking, and you say, Behold, a glutton and a wine-bibber' (Lk. vii. 33f. = Mt. xi. 18f.). It is possible, although the point cannot be pressed, that the use of the name 'Son of Man' by Jesus in a personal sense, with reference to himself, and not to a community, is significant. He has not renounced his belief in the Elect Community, but knows that as yet it is summed up in himself, its Head.

Even more revealing are the Woes on the Galilean towns recorded in Lk. x. 13–15 = Mt. xi. 21–24:

'Woe unto you, Chorazin! woe unto you, Bethsaida! for if the mighty works done in you had been done in Tyre and Sidon, they would have repented long ago, sitting in sackcloth and ashes. But it shall be more tolerable in the judgement for Tyre and Sidon than for you. And you, Capernaum, will you be exalted to heaven? you shall be brought down to Hades'.

Again, it is impossible, with any conviction, to assign these words to the period before the mission of the Twelve; they disclose the situation in Galilee as it was seen at some point after that event. Fruitless visits of Jesus to these towns, all within a comparatively short radius around the lake, are implied, which are not recorded in the Gospels. Luke connects the words with the mission of the Seventy (x. 1–12), but his arrangement is widely regarded as editorial. In Matthew they immediately follow the saying on the Son of Man quoted above, and are introduced by the words, 'Then began he to upbraid the cities where most of his mighty works had been done' (xi. 20). We have every reason to think that Jesus is referring to his own ministry. As through a dark window the saying points to poignant experiences on which he looked back with the keenest regret. C. J. Cadoux does not exaggerate when he says, 'Now if Jesus spoke in this way, and meant what he said, and was not simply indulging in meaningless stage-play or unintelligent fatalism, he was expressing real and passionate disappointment. No feasible alternative view is possible.  If these utterances do not evince a most poignant sense of frustration, they mean nothing'.[1]  In the existing state of the tradition it is impossible to date these sayings with any precision, but it may certainly be said that they are retrospective, implying an experience of fruitless activity in the closing days of the Galilean ministry.

What is the explanation of the frustration to which these sayings point?  Many writers of Lives of Christ have spoken of a waning of the popularity of Jesus with the people at this time, in consequence of which he withdrew from public teaching and devoted himself exclusively to the training and instruction of the disciples.  Certainly a little later he begins to instruct his disciples concerning Messianic suffering (cf. Mk. viii. 31, ix. 12, 31, x. 33f., 45); but of a declining popularity at this period there is no sign.  On the contrary, Herod Antipas is deeply concerned at the 'success' of Jesus (Mk. vi. 14–16), and when Jesus seeks retirement with his disciples across the Lake, crowds follow him from the adjacent towns and villages and precede the boat to the point of landing (Mk. vi. 30–4).  At the descent from the Mount of Transfiguration a great multitude surrounds the disciples (Mk. ix. 14f.), and later still, when he comes 'into the borders of Judaea and beyond Jordan', 'multitudes come together unto him again' (Mk. x. 1).  It is not a waning popularity which compels Jesus to regard the Galilean ministry as a failure, and which drives him into seclusion.  It is the popularity itself and, above all, its facile character.  The people do not repent and do not believe that the Kingdom of God is at hand.  The unreceptiveness of his generation appears to have astonished Jesus.  At Nazareth he had marvelled at their unbelief (Mk. vi. 5f.), and only a little

[1] *The Historic Mission of Jesus*, 192.

later he was to say, 'O faithless generation, how long am I to be with you? how long am I to bear with you?' (Mk. ix. 19). Here undoubtedly is expressed the feeling which determines the further course of his story.

# XXVI

# HEROD'S FEARS AND THE FATE
## OF JOHN THE BAPTIST

WHAT importance is to be attached to an alternative explanation of the withdrawal of Jesus at this period from public activity, the theory of 'a flight from Herod'? Several scholars have suggested various forms of this explanation. F. C. Burkitt suggested that after the fame of Jesus came to the ears of Antipas he was an object of suspicion at the court, and 'like David and Elijah in the old days, he was forced to leave the country'.[1] More recently M. Goguel has said that Herod's decision to kill Jesus makes a break in the story of the Galilean ministry. 'From that time forward', he says, 'Jesus was obliged to flee from place to place and sometimes to conceal himself altogether',[2] and further, 'It is because he feels himself a hunted man that Jesus only appears again in Galilee as a passer-by and leads a wandering life'.[3]

These views, which out-run the evidence, are based upon the stories of Herod's fears (Mk. vi. 14–16) and the murder of the Baptist (Mk. vi. 17–29) which precede the period of withdrawal. When Herod first began to take a political interest in the ministry of Jesus we do not know. Mark has placed the story of vi. 14–16 immediately after the mission of the Twelve. There is no close link between these stories, for it was not of the mission that Herod speculated, but of the activity of

---

[1] *The Gospel History and its Transmission*, 93f.
[2] *The Life of Jesus*, 359.      [3] *Op. cit.*, 364.

Jesus himself. The name of Jesus, Mark tells us, had become known. People were saying that he was John the Baptist risen from the dead, others that he was Elijah returned to earth, others again that he was a prophet like one of the old prophets. According to Mark, Herod himself took the first of these views, but probably he really meant 'It is John the Baptist all over again'. Luke brings this out when he pictures Herod saying, 'John I beheaded; but who is this concerning whom I hear these things?' (Lk. ix. 9). Luke adds significantly, 'And he sought to see him', and it is not necessary to amend this grim word, as Goguel suggests,[1] to 'sought to put him to death', in order to perceive Herod's mordant interest. Jesus was a marked man, a danger to the state.

Mark underlies this interest by relating the story of the murder of John which had happened some time before. He gives an account which, as Rawlinson has suggested,[2] was whispered darkly in the bazaars of Palestine, how that, stimulated by wine and wrought upon by the malice of Herodias his brother's wife, angered because of John's prophetic denunciation of their adultery, Herod murdered John at the request of a dancing girl. Josephus, the historian, gives a different explanation. He writes: 'Herod, who feared lest the great influence John had over the people might put it into his power and inclination to raise a rebellion (for they seemed ready to do anything he should advise), thought it best, by putting him to death, to prevent any mischief he might cause, and not bring himself into difficulties, by sparing a man who might make him repent of it when it should be too late'.[3] There is no need to regard the two accounts as contradictory. Herod is not the first tyrant to combine political expediency

---

[1] *Op. cit.*, 355.  [2] *The Gospel according to St. Mark*, 82.
[3] *Ant.*, xviii. 5. 2.

I

with profligate folly. Indeed, the words 'by sparing a man who might make him repent of it when it should be too late' are not inconsistent with the Markan statement, 'when he heard him he was much perplexed, but (nevertheless) heard him gladly' (vi. 20). The contrast, however, suggests that, if it had been Mark's intention to represent the withdrawal of Jesus as 'a flight from Herod', he would have stressed the political hostility of Antipas to John rather than his profligacy. As a matter of fact, it is Matthew who writes: 'When he heard (of the death of John) Jesus withdrew from thence in a boat to a wilderness place privately' (Mt. xiv. 13). Nowhere does Mark say anything of the kind, and this fact is significant since he associates the Herodians with the scribes in their hostility to Jesus (Mk. iii. 6, xii. 13).

The true attitude of Jesus to the threats of Herod comes out in Luke's story about certain Pharisees who bade him depart because Herod desired to kill him. 'Go and tell that fox', Jesus replied, 'Behold, I cast out daemons and perform cures to-day and to-morrow, and the third day I am perfected. Howbeit I must go on my way to-day and to-morrow and the day following, for it cannot be that a prophet perish out of Jerusalem' (Lk. xiii. 32f.). These are not the words of one who was likely to take to the hills as a fugitive for his own personal security.

In one respect only is it probable that Herod's hostility affected the plans of Jesus, namely, his perception that Messianic excitement might provoke his followers to armed revolt against Rome. C. J. Cadoux has made a valuable contribution to our understanding of the life of Jesus by his warning against undervaluing his teaching about the folly of revolution.[1] This teaching belongs

---

[1] *The Historic Mission of Jesus*, 163–74, 266–79.

to the closing stages of his ministry, but the danger can well have occupied his thoughts at this earlier period, and may have been one factor in leading to his withdrawal from Galilee. Bethsaida, it has often been pointed out, for which the disciples set out in the boat after the meal in the wilderness at the command of Jesus (Mk. vi. 45), lay outside the territory of Antipas. The fate of John was a pointer which could not be ignored. We are right to take every circumstance into account which may bear upon an undeniable change in the plans of Jesus at this time; but we go seriously astray unless we place first in importance, not his personal safety, nor counsels of prudence, but the failure of the people of Galilee to respond to the message and demand of the Kingdom as Jesus preached it.[1] This failure is the key to the obscure period in the ministry to which we have now come.

[1] Cf. C. H. Dodd, *A Companion to the Bible* (ed. T. W. Manson, 1939, 5th impression, 1947), p. 383, 'It is probable that the withdrawal from Galilee was due not simply to the menace of death from Herod and the Pharisees, but even more to the fact that the Galilean populace responded in the wrong way to the proclamation of the Kingdom of God. They surrounded Jesus with a mistaken enthusiasm, but did not "repent" '. Cf. also T. W. Manson, *The Servant-Messiah* (1953), 71, 'I regard this withdrawal as a flight, but far more a flight from the dangerous enthusiasm of his friends than from the suspicion and fears of his enemies'.

# XXVII

## THE FELLOWSHIP MEAL
## IN THE WILDERNESS

SHORTLY after the mission of the Twelve Jesus invited his disciples to retire to a wilderness place for rest (Mk. vi. 31). It is impossible not to infer that the two events were closely connected, although all that Mark says by way of explanation is that there were many coming and going and that they had not leisure even to eat. Did Jesus intend to discuss the mission and its results with them in seclusion? If this is so, the attempt was frustrated. The people saw them departing, and following them on foot from all the towns and villages met them at the place of landing, probably a locality on the north-east shore in the lonely neighbourhood between *Wady es-Samak* and *Wady-en-Nkeb*.[1] The narrative of Mk. vi. 30–34 suggests that Jesus was unable to resist the silent appeal of the crowd. In words strongly reminiscent of the Old Testament he saw them 'as sheep not having a shepherd', and he began to teach them at length. What the theme of his teaching was we are not told, but, in the light of the story of the meal, it is reasonable to infer that he spoke of the rule of God, and perhaps illustrated his teaching by such parables as the Lost Sheep, the Lost Coin, and the Lost Son (Lk. xv. 1–32).

Apparently, the teaching continued until the late afternoon until at length the disciples became alarmed about the physical needs of the people. 'The place is lonely', they said, 'and already the hour is late. Send

---

[1] Cf. G. Dalman, *Sacred Sites and Ways*, 173.

them away, in order that they may go into the surrounding hamlets and villages and buy for themselves something to eat'. When Jesus bade his disciples feed them, they replied somewhat sarcastically, 'Are we to go and buy two hundred pennyworth of bread and give them to eat?' Jesus inquired what food was available and commanded the people to seat themselves in companies of fifty and a hundred upon the green grass. He then took the loaves and fishes and gave thanks and broke them, bidding the disciples to distribute them. Finally, the broken pieces left over were gathered. The number of the men present is said to have been five thousand.

Such is the story. At a very early period the incident was interpreted as a miracle, although it is curious that the only indication of this in the narrative is the statement after the meal, 'And they all ate and were satisfied', together with the numbers mentioned.[1] Probably these features are embellishments of the original story, although, it should be added, many commentators think otherwise. In any case, and whatever may be thought of the miraculous element in the narrative, the significance of the incident for the life of Jesus lies elsewhere. That a real meal was eaten is implied by the previous conversation between Jesus and his disciples, but the manner in which the story is told, and especially the verbs 'blessed', 'broke', and 'gave', suggest that in some sense the meal was an anticipation of the Last Supper.[2] Schweitzer well describes it as 'an eschatological sacrament'.[3] The

---

[1] Matthew adds 'besides women and children' (xiv. 21).

[2] Cf. Mk. vi. 41 and xiv. 22.

[3] *Op. cit.*, 377f. This view should be distinguished from interpretations which see in the miracle of the loaves a prefiguration of the Christian Eucharist. Cf. G. H. Boobyer, *JTS*, N.S., iii. 161–71. A sacramental meal is described which is eschatological and lacks the connexion with the death of Christ found in Mk. xiv. 21–5.

significance of the story is that Jesus intended the meal to
be an anticipation and a pledge of the Messianic feast
which in Jewish thought was associated with the per-
fecting of the Kingdom of God. It is along these lines
that the story is interpreted by many New Testament
scholars. The interpretation is fully in line with the
importance attached to the Messianic feast in the Old
Testament (cf. Isa. xxv. 6) and in later Jewish writings,[1]
and with other definite references to it in the Gospels.
In Lk. xiv. 15 a guest who sat at meat with Jesus cries,
'Blessed is he that shall eat bread in the kingdom of God',
and at the Last Supper Jesus himself says, 'Truly I tell
you, I will no more drink of the fruit of the vine, until
that day when I drink it new in the kingdom of God'
(Mk. xiv. 25).[2] We are justified in inferring that the
Supper celebrated on the night in which he was betrayed
was literally a *Last* Supper, with a deeper significance
because it was eaten on the eve of the Crucifixion, and that
it had been preceded by other, and perhaps many, meals
of the kind when Jesus with his disciples looked forward
to the final establishing of God's rule. If we may consider the meal in the wilderness as a meal ending in an act
of this sacramental character, it is clear that, despite delay,
and in spite of the failure of the mission of the Twelve,
Jesus had not renounced his belief in the imminence of
the kingdom. It would surely come and of this certainty
the present meal was the pledge and seal.

[1] Cf. I Enoch lxii. 14, 2 Baruch xxix. 5ff., 4 Ezra vi. 51ff., Pirqe Aboth
iii. 20.

[2] See also Lk. xxii. 30, 'that you may eat and drink at my table in my
kingdom'.

# XXVIII

## THE LANDING AT GENNESARET

THE interpretation given to the meal in the wilderness is confirmed by the immediate sequel to it, especially as it is described in the Fourth Gospel. John says that, perceiving that the people were about to come and take him by force to make him king, Jesus withdrew again to the hills by himself (Jn. vi. 15). Although Mark does not make this statement his account is fully in harmony with it. He shows that Jesus was at pains to separate his disciples from the crowd, and says that, after he had taken leave of the people, he went to the hills to pray (Mk. vi. 45f.). From these passages we may infer that Jesus was conscious of a dangerous undercurrent of Messianic excitement stimulated, against his will, by his teaching and the meal which followed. Hopes had been kindled which might issue in armed revolt against which the Romans would be compelled to take action. Instead of the Kingdom of God would come the confusion of men. It was clearly necessary to send his disciples away in order later to teach them the way of Messianic suffering. That Jesus was conscious of a sense of crisis may perhaps be inferred from Mark's reference to prayer.

The account of what subsequently happened at Gennesaret is in complete harmony with this tragic situation. Driven south from Bethsaida, the disciples approached the western shore, when Jesus came upon them so suddenly that they thought his form was that of a ghost. All saw him and were terrified, but Jesus said to them, 'Be of good courage; it is I; be not afraid'. When Jesus entered the boat, the wind fell and they landed on the shore in the region from which they had originally started. How Jesus came upon them during the storm is a question on which modern readers of the story are not likely to agree. Mark's account is that Jesus walked on the water. Those who think that this detail is legendary can point to a still later development of the tradition in Mt. xiv. 28–33, in which Peter also walks upon the water. It is not unreasonable to conclude that doctrinal and homiletical interests have left their mark upon a tradition which was confused from the beginning in the circumstances of a dark wild night at sea. Mark tells us that the disciples were utterly astonished, and he explains this statement by saying that they had failed to understand the meaning of the loaves because their minds were blinded. Speculations do not carry us far in the vain task of sorting out the original facts. Far more important for the story of Jesus is the account of what happened at Gennesaret after they had moored the boat to the shore.

Intense excitement greeted the return of Jesus and his disciples. Mark says that the people 'ran throughout that whole region and began to bring sick people on their pallets where they heard that he was' (vi. 55). Laid down in the market-places, the sufferers sought to touch even the fringe of his garment, and as many as did so were made whole (vi. 56). The passage is a summary statement, but it leaves a vivid impression of originality. Nothing is said of a preaching tour or of public teaching, and it is possible that as Jesus passed through the towns and villages, he was accompanied by few of his disciples, if indeed by any of them. Apparently, he went from place to place to see the situation for himself. Loisy has con-

jectured that Jesus supposed that he would not be recognised, and meant, at the first opportunity, to continue his
journey to a region where he and his disciples would be in
peace and safety. He feared to attract the attention of
Herod by exciting the enthusiam of the people in a district so near to Tiberias.[1] Several points in this construction invite criticism, although, contrary to his usual
attitude to Loisy's views, Lagrange speaks of it with
relative approval.[2] Can Jesus have imagined that he
would not be recognised? Does not Mark's description
of the market-places suggest otherwise? And was he in
fear of the hostility of Herod? More solidly based is
the suggestion that he still meant to fulfil his frustrated
purpose of seeking a place of retirement.[3] If this is so,
what he saw in the plain of Gennesaret can only have
strengthened his purpose. His sojourn gave him the
opportunity to assess his popularity. There is reason to
infer that it was the enthusiastic, but mistaken, attitude of
the people to his person and message which drove him
from Galilee. He turned his back upon a facile popularity
which to him was failure. Either at this time or a little
later, he was faced in the same locality with a demand for
a sign from heaven to authenticate his message (Mk.
viii. 11–13). This demand he roughly rejected. Groan-
ing in spirit he said to the Pharisees who disputed with
him, 'Why does this generation seek a sign? Truly I
tell you, no sign shall be given to this generation'.[4] Mark
adds the brief comment that, leaving them, he entered
into the boat again and went away to the other side. All
the indications are that Jesus was driven from Galilee

---

[1] *Les Évangiles synoptiques*, i. 947f.
[2] *Évangile selon Saint Marc*, 178.          [3] Cf. Mk. vi. 31.
[4] In the parallel saying in Q (Lk. xi. 29 = Mt. xii. 39) the clause 'except
the sign of Jonah' is added, the implication being that the preaching is a
sufficient sign, in other words, that his message is self-authenticating.

by the results of his own ministry.   Just as, after his
baptism, he went away into the wilderness of Judaea, so
now he felt the need of a place of retreat where in communion with his Father, he might seek a new orientation
of his mission.

*PART THREE*

THE WITHDRAWAL FROM GALILEE

# XXIX

## THE DEPARTURE TO
## THE REGION OF TYRE

THE withdrawal from Galilee to the region of Tyre
is of the greatest importance for the understanding
of the ministry of Jesus.  But before this question
can be profitably considered, it is necessary to discuss a
manifest confusion in the primitive record in Mk. vi.
30–viii. 26.[1]

The geographical passages concerning the withdrawal
are Mk. vii. 24, 'And from there he arose and went away
to the region of Tyre',[2] and Mk. vii. 31, 'And again going
forth from the borders of Tyre, he came through Sidon
to the sea of Galilee, through the region of the Decapolis'.[3]
Between these two passages is the story of the Syro-
Phoenician woman (vii. 24b–30).  After the second follows
the account of the cure of the deaf mute (vii. 32–7) the
narrative of the Feeding of the Four Thousand (viii. 1–9,)
and its sequel in the three narratives of viii. 10–26.

It has long been observed that between Mk. vi. 30–vii.
37 and Mk. viii. 1–26 there is a remarkable parallelism.
In the first part of each of these sections a fellowship
meal is followed by the crossing of the lake and a controversy with the Pharisees, probably in the same locality.
This relationship may be indicated as follows:

[1] I have discussed this question in detail in *The Gospel according to St.
Mark*, Appendix C, pp. 628–32, 'The Relationship between Mk. vi.
30–vii. 37 and viii. 1–26'.

[2] Omitting 'and Sidon' with important MSS.

[3] The difficult phrases 'through Sidon' and 'through the region of the
Decapolis' are discussed later, p. 132f.

| A | B |
|---|---|
| 1. vi. 30–44, The Feeding of the Five Thousand. | 1. viii. 1–9, The Feeding of the Four Thousand. |
| 2. vi. 45–53, The Crossing to Gennesaret. | 2. viii. 10, The Crossing to Dalmanutha. |
| 3. vii. 1–23, A Controversy with the Pharisees. | 3. viii. 11–13, A Controversy with the Pharisees. |

In the two controversies the subject at issue is different; in A it is the question of defilement, in B the demand for a sign. To this extent the parallelism is broken. But the story of the Four Thousand and the subsequent Crossing (B1 and 2) is widely believed by commentators to be a duplicate of the story of the Five Thousand and the Crossing to Gennesaret (A1 and 2), and although the precise location of Dalmanutha is not known, it is generally held to have been on the west shore, in or near the plain of Gennesaret.[1] One important gain of the doublet-hypothesis is that the series, a meal, a crossing, and a controversy, is doubly attested in Mark, and must probably reflect a well remembered succession of events. As was suggested earlier,[2] vii. 1–23 (A3), is a purely topical collection of stories and sayings, which may belong to various periods in the Galilean ministry. This consideration predisposes us to give preference to viii. 11–13 (B3) as the sequel to the crossing, although it is by no means thereby excluded that some at least of the contents of vii. 1–23 may belong to the same period. If these suggestions are accepted, the original series of events is A1 and 2 followed by B3, that is, vi. 30–56 and viii. 11–13.

At what point after these events must we place the withdrawal into the region of Tyre (vii. 24b–30)? The

---

[1] Cf. *The Gospel according to St. Mark*, 360f.     [2] See p. 87f.

continuation of the table printed above may be useful for reference. It is as follows:

| A | B |
|---|---|
| 4. vii. 24–31, The Journey into the region of Tyre and the story of the Syro-Phoenician Woman. | 4. viii. 14–21, The Recrossing of the Lake (to Bethsaida) and the conversation on the leaven of the Pharisees and of Herod. |
| 5. vii. 32–7, The Journey continued and the Healing of the Deaf Mute. | 5. viii. 22–6, The Cure of the Blind Man near Bethsaida. |

The opening phrase in vii. 24–31, 'And from there', is so vague that it is possible to place the narrative either before or after viii. 11–13. Either the withdrawal immediately followed the stay at Gennesaret (vi. 45–56) or it happened later after the demand for a sign (viii. 11–13) and the recrossing to Bethsaida (viii. 22).[1] Between these alternatives there is no means of deciding; but, on the whole, the second view seems more probable.[2] If so, Jesus departs from Gennesaret after his refusal to give a sign, crosses to Bethsaida, and from Bethsaida withdraws across the border into the adjacent region of Tyre. Such appears to have been the most probable course of events.

It may be of advantage, while considering critical questions, to discuss the account of the return given in Mk. vii. 31 which is quoted above. Mark says that Jesus came 'through Sidon' to the sea of Galilee through the region of the Decapolis. Sidon stands on the coast some twenty miles north of Tyre. Thus a journey, which must have occupied several months, first north, then south east, and then south is described, a long detour across rivers

---

[1] Cf. J. Weiss, *Die Schriften des Neuen Testaments*, ed. 4, 140f.
[2] Cf. *The Gospel according to St. Mark*, 630–2.

and mountains which may have included a transit through Caesarea Philippi and the pagan regions north east and east of the lake. Rawlinson[1] compares the route to a journey from Cornwall to London *via* Manchester; Dalman[2] says that the reference to the district of the Decapolis should not be taken literally; and Blunt[3] declares that the geography is impossible. If we are not convinced that the purpose of the wanderings is to avoid the dominions of Antipas,[4] it is difficult to account for the journey, especially when only a little later Jesus is once more twenty-five miles north of Bethsaida in the villages of Caesarea Philippi (Mk. viii. 27). In these circumstances the conjecture of Wellhausen[5] that 'through Sidon' is a misrendering of an Aramaic original for 'to Bethsaida' is attractive, for a return to Bethsaida would eliminate the necessity of the long journey. Such conjectures are always open to question[6] but for the shorter route itself there is much to be said. It is inherently the more probable itinerary, since it calls for no defence or explanation. It brings Jesus back to the lake, to the very place to which earlier he had intended to send his disciples (vi. 45). In this locality the cure of the blind man is set (viii. 22–6), and in the same setting, or in the Decapolis itself, the cure of the deaf mute belongs (vii. 32–7). On this point much depends on the explanation we give to the phrase 'through the region of the Decapolis' (vii. 31). Dalman's opinion, that the reference should not be taken too literally, has been mentioned above. It may also be argued that, in

[1] *The Gospel according to St. Mark*, 101.
[2] *Sacred Sites and Ways*, 201
[3] *The Gospel according to Saint Mark*, 192.
[4] Cf. F. C. Burkitt, *The Gospel History and its Transmission*, 93.
[5] *Einleitung in die drei ersten Evangelien*, ed. 1, 37.
[6] Cf. W. F. Howard in Moulton's *Grammar of New Testament Greek*, ii. 471.

this geographical passage, Mark intended to suggest that the Feeding of the Four Thousand and its sequel (viii. 1–9, 22–6) took place in Gentile territory, and thus to hint at the idea of a ministry to the Gentiles, a representation which could not be carried out with precision because the facts did not warrant it, but which, none the less, would have been of the greatest interest and importance to his Roman readers.

No one would pretend that we can be sure about the details of the itinerary. All that is possible is an opinion upon the question whether the longer or the shorter journey is the more probable. This question is one of much interest, but it is not a vital issue. In any reconstruction of the course of events it remains true that the withdrawal to the region of Tyre is the essential link between the failure of the Galilean ministry and the account of the decisive day when, in the vicinity of Caesarea Philippi, Jesus asked his disciples the pointed question, 'Who do you say that I am?', and forthwith began to teach them that 'the Son of Man must suffer many things, and be rejected' (Mk. viii. 29–31). If this contention is sound, it is of the greatest importance to ask what was the significance of the withdrawal itself.

## XXX

## THE SIGNIFICANCE OF THE WITH-
## DRAWAL TO THE REGION OF TYRE

WHAT happened during the withdrawal to the region of Tyre and Sidon and how did it influence the course of the ministry of Jesus? If progress in a historical inquiry depends on asking the right questions, there can be few issues more important than this question. Unfortunately, Mark tells us very little indeed concerning this interlude. All he relates is that Jesus arose and went away to the region of Tyre, that 'he entered into a house, and would have no man know it', but that 'he could not be hid' (vii. 24). Then follows the story of the Syro-Phoenician woman (vii. 25–30) and the geographical passage already considered about his return to the sea of Galilee (vii. 31). There are, of course, good reasons for this brevity. Apparently, Mark's information concerning this period in the life of Jesus was very limited, and, as always, he makes little or no attempt to describe his inner thoughts. On the contrary, it would appear, he is preoccupied by a desire to suggest that at this time Jesus ministered to Gentiles. At the same time, he not only mentions the retirement itself, but pointedly refers to a secret withdrawal which against his will was frustrated. It may also be inferred that Jesus was alone, for the disciples are not mentioned. Matthew explicitly mentions their presence, and relates that when the woman made her request, they said, 'Send her away, for she is crying after us' (xv. 23). Arguments from silence are admittedly precarious, but it is so much Mark's habit to mention the presence of the disciples at important events that we are probably justified in concluding that he is following a tradition to the effect that during this retreat Jesus was alone. If this is so, we can understand why so little is recorded and must assume that subsequently Jesus told his disciples of the incident of the Syro-Phoenician woman.

Are we at liberty to go beyond what is written in seeking to estimate the significance of the withdrawal? Modern criticism has repeatedly been warned against the perils of 'psychologising', and it is a healthy warning in view of the many ambitious reconstructions which have been built upon the slenderest foundations. In this case, however, we are not without indications, additional to the story of the woman, which suggest that it must have been highly important in its effect upon the purpose of Jesus, as important indeed as the withdrawal into the wilderness of Judaea which preceded the Galilean ministry. Before the retirement to the region of Tyre there is no evidence, apart from Mk. ii. 19b–20, that Jesus definitely connected his mission, as the Son of Man, with Messianic suffering. The divine voice at his baptism, 'Thou art my beloved Son' (i. 11), reflects the influence of Isa. xlii. 2, but not that of Isa. liii, and all the stress in the preaching of the Galilean ministry is on the imminence of the Kingdom, but not upon the sufferings which might be entailed. Very soon after the withdrawal, and immediately afterwards if we accept the view that Mk. viii. 1–10 is a doublet of Mk. vi. 30–56, Jesus began to teach his disciples as they journeyed through the villages near Caesarea Philippi that 'the Son of Man must suffer, and be rejected' (Mk. viii. 31).

Mark appends a group of sayings upon the theme of sacrifice (viii. 34–8), and from this point onwards re-

peatedly mentions attempts of Jesus to describe his suffering ministry to his disciples (ix. 12, 31, x. 33f., 45). We
may, if we will, describe this representation as 'schematisation', but if we extend this characterisation beyond
a certain relative arrangement of the material, we reject
the only tradition we possess, and, it may be claimed, a
tradition marked by internal consistency and general
trustworthiness. If, however, the tradition in its broad
outlines is accepted, we have good reason to infer that,
whether or not the idea of Messianic suffering had presented itself to the mind of Jesus earlier, it was during the
withdrawal to the region of Tyre that, stimulated by the
failure of the Galilean ministry and of the mission of the
Twelve, it fructified and became a dominating idea which
determined all his future activities. Nor is this all. The
fate of the Baptist, the history of the prophets, the
hostility of Herod, and the enmity of the scribes and
Pharisees, all pointed to the fact that the issue of his
ministry was bound to be tragic. It is, however, characteristic of Jesus that he does not think of this fate as
historically inevitable. He believes it to be pre-ordained
in the counsels of God and adumbrated in the portraiture
of the Suffering Servant of Isa. liii.

At some point in his ministry such thoughts must have
clarified in the mind of Jesus, and no better place can be
suggested than the withdrawal to the region of Tyre.
A fuller consideration of this teaching must be deferred
until the account of the confession of Peter when it is
first announced. Meantime we must ask whether the story
of the Syro-Phoenician woman is in harmony with the
suggestion, which Mark does not make, that the withdrawal was for Jesus a season of spiritual illumination on
the issues of his mission.

How far Jesus went into the region of Tyre is not

indicated in the Markan account, but a definite crossing
of the border is clearly implied (vii. 24). Matthew's
narrative (xv. 21–8) appears to imply that Jesus did not
actually enter this region, for it states that the woman
came to Jesus 'from that region' (xv. 22); but this
representation may be occasioned by a reluctance to admit
that Jesus entered Gentile territory. In Mark's narrative
the location is precise: 'He arose and went away to the
region of Tyre' (vii. 24). Coupled with the statement
that he entered into a house and wanted no one to know of
it, the passage suggests a desire for privacy and reflection.
If we say that the thoughts of Jesus inevitably turned to
the Galilean ministry, the preaching of the Kingdom, the
mission of the Twelve, the attitude of the people, and the
delay in the establishing of the Elect Community, we are
indulging in speculation. And yet, it may be claimed, not in
idle speculation. His words to the woman reveal the direction
of his thoughts. 'Let the children first be filled', he said,
'for it is not meet to take the children's bread and cast it to the
dogs' (vii. 27). These words suggest that Jesus was preoccupied with the thought of his mission to the Jews; and
it is to this tension that the apparent harshness of his
words is due. The reference to bread recalls the meal in
the wilderness and his conversation with the disciples in
the boat about leaven (viii. 15ff.). This inference is still
more strongly based if it was on the same occasion that he
said, 'I was not sent but unto the lost sheep of the house of
Israel' (Mt. xv. 24), and it is in favour of this association
that they immediately recall the Markan statement which
precedes the meal in the wilderness, 'He had compassion
on them, because they were like sheep without a shepherd'
(Mk. vi. 34). May we not dare to say that, when Jesus
spoke to the woman, he was also speaking to himself? And
do we not lose the key to the incident if we question the

originality of the word 'first'?  The suggestion of the
narrative is that Jesus said something to encourage the
woman's reply, in which with insight and daring she
carries his thought a stage farther.  Emboldened by his
reference to household dogs and his use of the word
'first', she continues, 'And, sir, the dogs under the table
eat of the children's crumbs'.  Jesus was delighted by her
wit.  'For this word', he said, 'go your way; the daemon
has left your daughter'—a confident assurance based on
supernatural knowledge, and not necessarily a miracle
wrought at a distance.

Mark has no other story to tell, and his silence is not
surprising if Jesus was alone at the time.  If we conclude
that he returned to his disciples with tension relieved and
a solution reached, it is because we are justified in drawing
this inference in the light of the confession of Peter and the
teaching which followed.  It was manifestly not enough
to summon men to repent, not enough to await God's
good pleasure in the giving of the Kingdom, true though
it was that the Kingdom is God's gift (Lk. xii. 32).  He
himself had a suffering destiny to fulfil before the gift
could be given.  With such thoughts in mind, we may
believe, he left Tyrian country.  He had great things to
impart to his disciples.  It may not be fanciful to suppose
that when later he said to the deaf man 'Ephphatha'
('Be opened'), and to the blind man, 'Do you see anything?', he was thinking of his disciples, and perhaps even
of himself.

## XXXI

## THE CONFESSION OF PETER

SOON after his return from the region of Tyre Jesus
came with his disciples into the villages round about
Caesarea Philippi, a town situated at the source of the
Jordan on the slopes of Mount Hermon. As they
journeyed he questioned his disciples regarding the
popular opinions concerning himself. 'Who do men say
that I am?', he asked. It is surprising that in the answers
given—John the Baptist, Elijah, one of the prophets—
there is no indication that he had generally been recognised as the Messiah. Apparently, Messianic excitement
ran as an undercurrent among his more immediate
disciples rather than among the mass of the people.
Nevertheless, after the meal in the wilderness, and probably also in Gennesaret, Jesus had seen a dangerous
situation, tinder which at a flash might leap into flame.
It was manifestly necessary that the disciples should learn
a new conception of Messiahship, a conception which, if
we have rightly interpreted the withdrawal to the region
of Tyre, had recently been present to his own mind. It
was in order to introduce this teaching that he so directly
asked, 'But who do you say that I am?' Characteristically,
Peter answered for the rest. 'You are the Messiah', he
replied.

No sooner had Peter made this confession than Jesus
laid a ban upon his disciples to tell no man of him (Mk.
viii. 30). Matthew correctly interprets the charge by
adding 'that he was the Messiah' (Mt. xvi. 20). There is
no need to question the historical character of this in-

junction; it accords completely with the situation. Jesus saw that Peter's declaration needed correction rather than praise.[1]   The confession was politically dangerous and misleading from the religious standpoint because it interpreted his Messiahship in terms of current expectations.   We are entitled to infer this because Jesus at once begins to teach a new and startling conception of Messiahship and because, when Peter hears the teaching, he is dumbfounded and affronted.   Manifestly, when Peter says, 'You are the Messiah', he means that Jesus is the divinely appointed Davidic leader and king.   Mark says that Jesus 'began to teach them that the Son of Man must suffer many things, and be rejected by the elders and the chief priests and the scribes, and be killed, and after three days rise again' (viii. 31).   The meaning and historical character of this teaching must be considered separately in the next section.   Here it is enough to note the incredulity with which it was greeted.

Mark bluntly says that Peter took him and began to rebuke him (viii. 32) and the same attitude is described by Matthew in direct speech.   'God forbid, Lord!', Peter cries, 'This shall never happen to you' (Mt. xvi. 22). Both Evangelists record the severity of the reply of Jesus: 'Get behind me, Satan: you do not think God's thoughts, but the thoughts of men' (Mk. viii. 33).   To question the historical character of such a story is hypercriticism.   The

[1] Matthew says that Jesus pronounced Peter blessed because he had received so great a revelation (xvi. 17).   He then adds the sayings on the rock on which the Church is built, the keys of the kingdom, and the power of binding and loosing (xvi. 18f.), the last named being a promise of forbidding and permitting in matters of moral conduct subsequently made to all the disciples (xviii. 18).   This account reflects later doctrinal and ecclesiastical interests.   The first question of Jesus is given in the form, 'Who do men say that the Son of Man is?' (xv. 13), and to Peter's confession the words 'the Son of the living God' are added, while the sayings serve to enhance his authority.

realism is that of fact, for who in the primitive Church would have invented such a crushing retort? It is clear that the foresight of Jesus had been amply justified. His closest disciples did expect him to be a Davidic Messiah, a leader of national revolt. It ought not to surprise us that the teaching on Messianic suffering had subsequently to be repeated more than once (cf. Mk. ix. 12, 31, x. 33f., 45) and that the disciples failed to comprehend it. So great is the inhibiting power of inherited and accepted ideas!

Mk. viii. 31 and the allied passages do not exhaust the teaching of Jesus on suffering and sacrifice. With good literary judgement Mark follows his account of the teaching with excerpts from his sayings-source which are appropriate to this period. 'If any man would come after me', said Jesus, 'let him deny himself and take up his cross and follow me' (viii. 34). To save one's life, he taught, is to lose it, to lose it for his sake is to save it. 'What does it profit a man, to gain the whole world', he asked, 'and to forfeit his life? For what can a man give in return for his life?' (viii. 36f.). These sayings show that, whatever Messianic suffering might entail for himself, there was in his view a part in it which his disciples must share. So closely bound up with his purpose and ministry is the teaching he began to give that we must consider it carefully and the problems it raises.

# XXXII

## MESSIANIC SUFFERING

Two questions regarding this teaching call for consideration: (1) its implications, especially the question of its relationship to the ideas of Isa. liii; and (2) its genuineness. Both questions are intimately bound up with the purpose and ministry of Jesus.

A close connexion between the teaching that the Son of Man 'must suffer' and Isa. liii is generally affirmed, both by those who accept it as a genuine element in the teaching of Jesus and by those who trace its origin to the work of the Christian community. Only in Lk. xxii. 37, 'For I tell you that this which is written must be fulfilled in me, And he was reckoned with transgressors', is Isa. liii expressly quoted; but its ideas seem unmistakably latent in Mk. viii. 31, ix. 12, 31, x. 33f., 45, xiv. 24, and Lk. xvii. 25. The basic conjunction of ideas in the prophecies of the Passion, suffering, rejection, death, and exaltation, is paralleled in Isa. liii. 3, 'He was despised, and rejected of men; a man of sorrows, and acquainted with grief'; liii. 4, 'Surely he hath borne our griefs, and carried our sorrows', coupled with the reference to the Servant as 'stricken' and 'afflicted'; liii. 8, 'By oppression and judgement he was taken away'; liii. 10, 'It pleased the Lord to bruise him; he hath put him to grief'; liii. 12, 'Because he poured out his soul unto death, and was numbered with the transgressors'. The vicarious element in Mk. x. 45 ('a ransom *for many*') and Mk. xiv. 24 ('my blood . . . which is shed *for many*') is also paralleled in Isa. liii. 5, 'He was wounded for our transgressions'; liii. 6,

'The Lord hath laid on him the iniquity of us all'; liii. 10, 'When thou shalt make his soul an offering for sin'; liii. 11, 'justify *many*'; and liii. 12, 'Yet he bare the sin of *many*, and made intercession for the transgressors'.

It will be seen that no saying, except Lk. xxii. 37 actually quotes Isa. liii, but the debt is surely unmistakable. The allusive character of the sayings corresponds to the manner in which in general Jesus draws upon the Old Testament. It suggests that he does not take the idea of Messianic suffering directly from Isa. liii, as a modern commentator might, but rather that from his own experience and insight he formulates this teaching and finds in the idea of the Suffering Servant the medium for its expression. This consideration robs of much of its force the fact that the text of Isa. liii. 10, as we now read it, is uncertain or corrupt.

But are the sayings genuine? Can we rely upon them as evidence for the mind and purpose of Jesus? Radical criticism answers these questions in the negative. 'Can there be any doubt', asks Bultmann almost without argument, 'that they are all *vaticinia ex eventu*?'.[1] His view is that the prophecies are the work of the Hellenistic Christian community.[2] The prophecies, Bultmann argues, do not speak of the Parousia, while the Son of Man sayings which have to do with the Parousia do not mention suffering, and the former are not found in Q.[3] Neither argument is convincing. The absence of the prophecies from Q could occasion surprise only if there were good reason to expect them in Q. Further, the lack

---

[1] *The Theology of the New Testament*, 29.

[2] *Op. cit.*, 30. The view that the prophecies are due to dogmatic redaction is maintained by Wrede, *Das Messiasgeheimnis in den Evangelien*, 88ff., Bousset, *Kyrios Christos*, 9, 16n, 24n, 65n, 71n, and others, and recently by E. Percy, *Die Botschaft Jesu*, 240–5.

[3] *Op. cit., ibid.*

of references to the Parousia still needs to be explained if they are community-sayings, especially since the expectation of the End was so prominent in primitive Christianity.   Moreover, as earlier maintained,[1] the mutual segregation of the Passion-sayings and the Parousia-sayings is not surprising, if many of the latter belong to the early Galilean ministry.   The strongest objection to the communal origin of the prophecies is that this explanation is less tenable than the hypothesis of their originality. Communities do not create sayings;[2] still less do they creatively combine diverse ideas like the Son of Man and the Suffering Servant of Isa. liii.   Such combinations[3] are made by the insight of individuals.   If this is so, no good reason can be given why this teaching should not have originated with Jesus himself.   Bultmann recognises that the ideas of Ac. viii. 32f., I Pet. ii. 22–5, and Heb. ix. 28 'may be older than Paul', says that Rom. iv. 25 is 'probably a saying quoted by Paul',[4] and frequently endorses the view of Lohmeyer that Phil. ii. 6–11 is a pre-Pauline hymn.[5]   The possibility that some unknown thinker first interpreted the Passion in terms of Isa. liii cannot antecedently be ruled out, but that Jesus first so interpreted the necessity and meaning of his death is far more probable.[6]   Even if the idea of a suffering Messiah was present in some degree in pre-Christian Judaism,[7] it would still be true that Jesus made it current coin.

The character of the sayings supports this claim.   Only Mk. x. 33f., by its detail, reflects a knowledge of the

---

[1] See earlier p. 73
[2] Cf. B. S. Easton, *The Gospel before the Gospels*, 116f.
[3] Cf. W. Manson, *Jesus the Messiah*, 110–19, 128–34.
[4] *Op. cit.*, 31.          [5] *Op. cit.*, 125, 131, 175, 232.
[6] Cf. J. Jeremias, *KThW*, v. 711, who says that this view has strong historical probability (*starke historische Wahrscheinlichkeit*).
[7] Cf. J. Jeremias, *KThW*, v. 697f.

Passion story, although possibly the phrase 'after three days' in Mk. ix. 31 has replaced a more general allusion to triumph and exaltation. Mk. ix. 12, 'And how is it written of the Son of Man, that he should suffer many things and be set at naught', and Lk. xvii. 25, 'But first must he suffer many things and be rejected by this generation', are not even open to this charge,[1] and Mk. x. 45, 'The Son of Man . . . came to give his life a ransom for many', is certainly not Pauline. The sayings, it may be claimed, have a genuine ring.

A point of importance is the fact that Mark represents this teaching as private instruction given to the disciples. This representation is natural and in no way needs to be explained as an editorial device. It is only what might be expected that Jesus should set the teaching before the disciples first, and credible that he should say that they too would share his suffering (Mk. x. 38). Nor can it be thought strange that the disciples found such teaching hard to apprehend. Only the logic of events could make it plain.

[1] Cf. R. Otto, *The Kingdom of God and the Son of Man*, 247, 249–61, 361–3.

# XXXIII

# THE TRANSFIGURATION

Six days after the confession of Peter Jesus took with him Peter, James, and John, and led them up into a high mountain apart from the rest of the disciples (Mk. ix. 2). This temporal statement has no parallel in the Gospel of Mark except in the reference to 'two days' before the Passover in xiv. 1 and in the allusions to days and hours in the week preceding the Passion. Since these passages are meant to be taken as chronological, it is natural to interpret ix. 2 in the same way. There is no need to explain the 'six days' as a symbolic number reminiscent of the Feast of Tabernacles[1] or of the period during which Moses tarried on the mount of God before the divine voice called to him from the cloud (cf. Ex. xxiv. 15f.).[2] The statement implies that the interval which separated the incident from Peter's confession was remembered. The high mountain is not named. The tradition that it was Mount Tabor is not likely to be correct, for this hill is situated ten miles south-west of the Sea of Galilee and rises only to a thousand feet. Most commentators identify it with Mount Hermon, which is 9,200 feet high and is twelve miles to the north-east of Caesarea Philippi.

It is not possible for the modern reader to be at all sure what actually happened on the mountain, for much is left unrelated, and along with factual statements there are points in the narrative which reflect a doctrinal interest.

[1] Cf. A. Farrer, *A Study in Mark*, 214f.
[2] Cf. E. Lohmeyer, *Das Evangelium des Markus*, 173.

The narrative is not a post-resurrection story read back into the life of Jesus, for this interpretation leaves the references to Moses and Elijah unexplained. A more probable explanation is the view that, in the earliest tradition, the incident was regarded as an anticipation of Christ's Parousia, and that the story was told from this standpoint. The statement that Jesus 'was transfigured' and the allusions to the unearthly whiteness of his garments, to the cloud, and to the divine voice, point in this direction.[1] On this interpretation the symbolic elements in the narrative are due to the religious interests it was meant to serve. This explanation, however, only partially accounts for the narrative, for there are indications that it rests on a basis of remembered fact. Characteristically Peter cries, 'Rabbi, it is good for us to be here: let us make three tents, one for you and one for Moses and one for Elijah' (Mk. ix. 5). The use of the name 'Rabbi' and the impulsive request leave upon the mind a strong impression of authenticity, and the comment of the Evangelist, 'He did not know what to say, for they were exceedingly afraid', is entirely natural.

The growing tendency among New Testament scholars to urge that we must remain content with what the Evangelists relate is pertinent in the case of a narrative so obscure as that of the Transfiguration. If, however, we are not willing to acquiesce in this historical reserve, it is necessary to resort to conjecture on the basis of what is recorded. The inwardness of the experience of Jesus himself is beyond analysis, but from the narrative and from his habit of retiring from men for prayer[2] it is permissible to infer that the rapture of communion with his

---

[1] Cf. G. H. Boobyer, *St. Mark and the Transfiguration Story*, 64–86.
[2] Cf. Mk. i. 35, vi. 46, xiv. 35, 39; Lk. iii. 21, v. 16, vi. 12, ix. 18, 28f., xi. 1, xxii. 41, 44.

Father was visible in his face.  To go further, as many
writers have done, and to say that his divine 'essential
form' (Phil. ii. 6) broke through the limitations of his
human body, is a theological interpretation, which may be
valid, but which cannot be inferred directly from the
narrative itself.

To explain the experience of the disciples is impossible
if psychological explanations are not permitted, and these
are necessarily precarious.  Luke is the first interpreter to
tread this path.  'Now Peter and they that were with him
were heavy with sleep', he writes, 'but when they were
fully awake, they saw his glory and the two men that were
with him' (ix. 32).[1]  These statements are either the inferences of Luke himself or views already current in the
tradition.  All that Mark says is that 'suddenly looking
around they no longer saw any one with them but Jesus
only' (ix. 8), and we do well to accept his reserve.  The
reference to the heaviness of sleep is not incredible, and
it is possible that, stimulated by the sight of Jesus in the
rapture of prayer, the disciples saw a vision, accompanied
by auditory and visible phenomena elsewhere well
attested in the experiences of saints and mystics.[2]  In
these matters we have to confess our ignorance, and only
tentative suggestions are possible.  The main points
which emerge from the narratives are the illumination
which came to Peter and his companions on the mountain
after the days of tension which followed the stern rebuke
of Jesus near Caesarea Philippi, and the deeper conviction
which they now received that Jesus was indeed the
Messiah, God's Beloved Son.  In another manner this
conviction is expressed in the Matthaean saying: 'Blessed

[1] Luke also says that Moses and Elijah 'appeared in glory' and spoke of
'his departure which he was to accomplish at Jerusalem' (ix. 31).
[2] Cf. Ed. Meyer, *Ursprung und Anfänge des Christentums*, i. 152–6.

are you, Simon Bar-Jonah! For flesh and blood did not reveal it unto you, but my Father who is in heaven' (xvi. 17).

Descending from the mountain, the disciples faced the problems which their conviction raised. It is not surprising that Jesus laid a ban of silence upon the three until the Son of Man should have risen from the dead (Mk. ix. 9). But they questioned among themselves what 'when he should rise again from the dead' might mean. How was the scribal view, that Elijah must come first, to be interpreted? Jesus admitted the truth of this expectation, but with the patience of a teacher recalled their attention to the far more important question, 'How is it written of the Son of Man, that he should suffer many things and be set at nought?'. Elijah, he declared, had come, and men had done to him what they willed, as it was written of him. This cryptic remark is correctly interpreted by Matthew in the words, 'Then understood the disciples that he spoke unto them of John the Baptist' (xvii. 13). F. C. Burkitt,[1] I believe, was fully justified in claiming that Mk. ix. 9–13 reads 'like reminiscences of a real conversation'. At the foot of the mountain the nine remaining disciples were engaged in a vain attempt to restore an epileptic lad, who foamed at the mouth, ground his teeth, and pined away. Few more dramatic contrasts can be imagined!

[1] *Christian Beginnings*, 33f.

L

*PART FOUR*

THE JERUSALEM MINISTRY

# XXXIV

## THE JOURNEY TO JERUSALEM

SOME time after the Confession of Peter and the
Transfiguration Jesus with his disciples began the
journey through Samaria and Judaea to Jerusalem
which was to end with his death. The journey appears
to have been made with many halts and interruptions.
Mark's account is very summary and reveals a want of
detailed information, which is only partially met by the
fuller, but disjointed, account in Lk. ix. 51–xviii. 14.
Presumably with reference to the neighbourhood of
Caesarea, Mark says 'they went forth from thence, and
passed through Galilee' (ix. 30), and, after mentioning
Capernaum in ix. 33, says 'He arose from thence and
came into the region of Judaea and beyond Jordan' (x. 1).
Incidentally he alludes to the journey in x. 17 in the
phrase 'in the way', when introducing the story of the
rich man who asked how he might inherit eternal life,
and more expressly in x. 32 in the words, 'And they were
in the way, going up to Jerusalem'. Finally, he tells us,
Jesus and his disciples passed through Jericho (x. 46),
and approached Jerusalem by way of Bethphage and
Bethany (xi. 1). The memory of this journey has left its
mark on the Gospel tradition, but no detailed information is available.

Luke makes the departure to Jerusalem a turning point
in his story, when he writes, 'And it came to pass, when
the days drew near for him to be received up, that he set
his face to go to Jerusalem, and sent messengers before
him' (ix. 51), and he has further allusions to the journey in

xiii. 22, xvii. 11, and xix. 11.  It has been conjectured that Lk. ix. 51–xviii. 14 is an independent account of the journeys of Jesus, the first in ix. 51–xi. 13, the second in xiii. 1–34 subsequent to the mission of the Twelve and the hostility of Herod, and the third in xvii. 11–xviii. 14 after a sojourn in the territory of Herod Philip,[1] but it is doubtful if this ingenious construction can be relied upon.[2]    The truth is the tradition has preserved little more than single stories for this period in the ministry of Jesus.

The purpose of the journey to Jerusalem has been variously estimated.    Thus, by many writers it has been described as 'a journey to death', and by others as a missionary progress undertaken to begin a teaching ministry in Jerusalem.    These alternatives are not necessarily mutually exclusive.    Jesus knew that his ministry in Jerusalem might end in death, as his saying, 'It cannot be that a prophet perish out of Jerusalem' (Lk. xiii. 33) shows, but the fact that he did carry on a teaching ministry there, engaging in controversy with the scribes and Pharisees, indicates his conviction that the holy city must be given the opportunity to face the challenge of his message.

It is credible that the first part of his journey through Galilee was made in secrecy: 'He would not that any man should know it' (Mk. ix. 30).    The Galilean ministry had ended and Jesus sought to teach his disciples the truth of Messianic suffering (Mk. ix. 31).    It is a possible view that the three predictions of the Passion (Mk. viii. 31, ix. 31, x. 33f.) are variants of the same tradition.    If so, the tradition is triply attested.    But it is more probable, I believe, that this teaching, so strange to Jewish ears, had

[1] Cf. L. Girard, *L'Évangile des voyages de Jesus* (1951).
[2] Cf. C. F. Evans, *JTS*, N.S., iii. 242–6.

to be repeated not once nor twice, and certainly the statement that 'they understood not the saying, and were
afraid to ask him' (Mk. ix. 33) is natural and gives
individuality to the scene.

At Capernaum Jesus gave his disciples a much needed
lesson on humility. He had observed them disputing in
the way who was the greatest, and sitting down he said to
them, 'If any man would be first, he shall be last of all,
and servant of all' (Mk. ix. 35). The statement that he
set a little child in the midst of them, taking him in his
arms, may be a variant of the story of the Blessing of the
Children (Mk. x. 13–16), but similar incidents are not
necessarily the same, and the dramatic use of a child as an
example of humility is distinctive of the earlier story. In
this teaching we stand near the bedrock of the tradition,
for apart from the parallels to Mk. ix. 35 in Mt. xviii. 3,
xxiii. 11, and Lk. ix. 48b there are similar sayings in Mk.
x. 43f., with parallels in Mt. xx. 26f. and Lk. xxii. 26 and,
as regards humility, in the two doublets in Mt. xviii. 4 and
xxiii. 12 and in Lk. xiv. 11 and xviii. 14. Characteristic indeed of the teaching of Jesus is the saying, 'Truly I tell you,
Except you turn, and become as little children, you shall in
no wise enter into the kingdom of heaven' (Mt. xviii. 3).

The sayings which follow in Mk. ix. 37–50 cannot be
dated or placed with certainty in any outline of the story
of Jesus, for they have clearly been taken from a collection
provided with mnemonic links to assist catechetical
instruction. All that we can say is that the story of the
strange exorcist, who was casting out daemons in the name
of Jesus, but was not a disciple of his, belongs to a
relatively late period in the ministry of Jesus, and that the
command 'Forbid him not' is part of that training of the
disciples to which after the Galilean ministry Jesus
appears to have devoted himself.

From Galilee Jesus came into Samaria. Of this part of the journey Mark records nothing, but Luke tells the story of the inhospitable Samaritan village, of the desire of James and John to call down fire from heaven to consume them, and of the rebuke of Jesus, ending with the simple statement, 'they went to another village' (Lk. ix. 51–6). Most of all do we feel the lack of chronological information in our primary authorities at this stage in the journey, due to their lack of a biographical interest, and the temptation to imagine situations for sayings and parables must in consequence be resisted.

So exceptional is Mark's statement that Jesus 'comes into the region of Judaea and beyond Jordan' (x. 1) that it claims attention. Some manuscripts omit the conjunction 'and' in this passage, thus producing a reading which is unintelligible, while others replace 'and' by 'through'. The latter reading is probably a scribal gloss, but it may be a correct interpretation of Mark's meaning: Jesus came to Judaea, but by way of Peraea on the east side of the Jordan. F. C. Burkitt[1] conjectured that, along with James and John, Jesus journeyed south, through Samaria, while Peter and the rest went through Peraea. The advantage of this conjecture is that it explains the reading 'into the region of Judaea beyond Jordan', which Burkitt accepts, as reflecting the standpoint of Peter on the east side of the river. Further, it avoids the necessity of bringing Jesus into Peraea, which belonged to the territory of Antipas. It also accounts for the want of detail in Mark's narrative, since Jesus and Peter travelled by different routes. Against the conjecture is the greater probability of the alternative reading 'and beyond Jordan', and the fact that Jesus did not need to avoid Peraea, since he had already passed through Galilee, although secretly.

[1] Cf. *The Gospel History and its Transmission*, 96f.

The suggestion, therefore, which Burkitt does not claim to be more than a conjecture, does not seem necessary. In particular, the want of precise detail is due, not so much to the temporary absence of Peter, but to the want of a biographical interest on the part of the Evangelist.

Lacking topographical and chronological information, Mark appears to have assembled Pronouncement-stories and sayings topically, as he does in ii. 1–iii. 6, iii. 19b–35, and vii. 1–23, without connecting-links other than the phrases, 'multitudes came together again', and 'as he was going forth into the way' (x. 1, 17). We see how impossible it is for the modern scholar to give a day to day account of the journey to Jerusalem, if he refuses to read too much 'between the lines', as, for example, by adopting the gratuitous suggestion that the little one Jesus took into his arms (x. 16) was Peter's child. We see also how the single story, rather than the continuous narrative, has been preserved best in the earliest tradition. Not without skill Mark records stories about divorce, children, eternal life, wealth, and rewards (x. 2–30), which are of greater value to us than precise information about the course of the journey, much as we may desire to possess such knowledge. All that we can say concerning the route is that Jesus probably followed 'the pilgrim way' to Jerusalem, with many halts and interruptions, resuming on occasion public teaching in parables, sayings, and controversies, but in the main instructing his disciples.

# XXXV
# THE APPROACH TO JERUSALEM

A STRIKING passage in Mk. x. 32 compensates in some degree for the want of detail in Mark's account of the approach of Jesus and his disciples to Jerusalem: 'And they were in the way, going up to Jerusalem; and Jesus was going before them: and they were amazed; and they that followed were afraid'. The Evangelist's intention is to represent Jesus pressing ahead in a manner which filled the disciples with a sense of awe. Only rarely does he describe the emotions of Jesus, his anger, his indignation, and his sighing, and perhaps nowhere to a degree comparable with this passage, with the exception of the statement that he began to be 'greatly amazed and sore troubled' in the story of Gethsemane. The passage is even more striking if we accept the interesting conjecture of C. H. Turner[1] and read the singular, 'And he was amazed'. We then lose the strange distinction between the disciples and 'they that followed' and perceive more clearly that the fear or awe of the disciples is inspired by the bearing and resolute lead of Jesus.

The passage introduces the third prophecy of the Passion (x. 33f.), which more than viii. 31 and ix. 31 reflects, as we have recognised,[2] the circumstances described in the Passion Narrative—the delivering up of Jesus to the chief priests and scribes, his condemnation, surrender to the Romans, mocking, scourging, death, and resurrection. A clear 'prophecy after the event', the

---

[1] Cf. Turner, *The Gospel according to St. Mark*, 50f.
[2] See earlier, p. 144f.

narrative appears to have been constructed by the
Evangelist, but, unless we are prepared to credit him
with a flight of historic imagination, the opening words,
mentioned above, reflect the testimony of an eyewitness.
In such a context the prophecy is appropriately introduced, illustrating the manner in which his impending
Messianic suffering filled the mind of Jesus at this time.

No less in keeping with the circumstances is the story of
the ambitious request of James and John (x. 35–45),
which, although probably current in the tradition as an
isolated story, is introduced with great art at this point.  A
story which does James and John no credit, the narrative
cannot be attributed to pious imagination.  On the
contrary, it must be derived from the best tradition.
'Grant unto us', said the two disciples, 'to sit, one at your
right hand, and one at your left, in your glory'.  The
request clearly reflects the preoccupations which made the
teaching concerning Messianic suffering so difficult to
credit and so hard to impart.  That Jesus was thinking
of this suffering is reflected by his reply.  'Are you able',
he asked, 'to drink the cup that I drink, or to be baptised
with the baptism with which I am baptised?' (x. 38).
When they replied that they were able, he declared that
they should drink his cup and share his baptism, but
added in words that cannot have been invented: 'But
to sit at my right hand or at my left is not mine to give,
but is for those for whom it has been prepared'.

The suggestion that Jesus is prophesying the martyr-
dom of James and John, in harmony with a statement
doubtfully ascribed to Papias,[1] misses the spirit and inten-

---

[1] The saying reported by Philip of Side, 'John the divine and James his
brother were killed by the Jews'.  Recently W. L. Knox has observed that
its acceptance 'involves a quite monumental preference for the inferior
evidence', *The Sources of the Synoptic Gospels*, i. 71f.

tion of the words of Jesus, in which he associates his disciples with his Messianic suffering. His saying on cross-bearing (Mk. viii. 34) points in the same direction, as also his action later when he separated Peter, James and John from the rest of the disciples and took them with him into the garden of Gethsemane (Mk. xiv. 33). That this teaching survived in the memory of primitive Christianity is reflected in the words of St. Paul, 'I fill up on my part that which remains over of the afflictions of Christ in my flesh for his body's sake, which is the church' (Col. i. 24).

Mark connects with this story a narrative concerning the indignation of the remaining ten disciples which Luke includes in his account of the conversation which followed the Last Supper (Lk. xxii. 24–7). It may have been an isolated story in the tradition, but it is equally possible that Mark gives it its original position. 'They began to be indignant', he says, 'at James and John' (x. 41). All the interest in the story is concentrated in the reply of Jesus, in which he re-iterates his teaching concerning true greatness (cf. ix. 35). 'You know that those who are supposed to rule over the Gentiles lord it over them, and their great men exercise authority over them. But it shall not be so among you: but whoever would be great among you shall be your servant, and whoever would be first among you shall be the slave of all'. Luke adds the saying, 'I am in the midst of you as he that serveth' (xxii. 27), but Mark ends his narrative with the words, 'For verily the Son of Man came not to be served, but to serve, and to give his life a ransom for many' (x. 45). This saying cannot be dismissed as Pauline, for neither the thought nor the vocabulary is characteristic of St. Paul. The words, in which the phrase 'for many' recalls Isa. liii. 12, stand or fall with the Servant teaching implicit in the sayings of Jesus concerning his death, and there are sound reasons, I believe, for accepting them as genuine.[1] The reference to deliverance in the word 'ransom' is metaphorical, and the metaphor is used to express an arresting thought. It expresses far more than the idea of self-sacrifice. Jesus speaks as the head of a redemptive community especially of himself, but not without regard to his followers. As he draws near to Jerusalem he knows that he must suffer on behalf of, and in the name of, men. This suffering is his cup and baptism.

At Jericho, some fifteen miles from the city, an incident happened which evidently left a deep impression on the minds of eyewitnesses. A blind beggar, the son of Timaeus, sitting by the roadside, began to cry out when he heard that Jesus of Nazareth was passing by, 'Jesus, Son of David, have pity on me'. Undeterred by the rebukes of many, he cried all the more, 'Son of David, have pity on me'. The address cannot have been welcome to Jesus, but unable to resist the appeal of suffering, he stopped and summoned the man to come to him. Throwing aside his cloak, the blind man sprang up and came to him, asking for the recovery of his sight. 'Go your way', said Jesus, 'your faith has restored you'. 'And immediately', Mark writes, 'he received his sight and followed him in the way'. The story of Zacchaeus, which Luke connects with Jericho, illustrates once more the sympathy of Jesus for the outcast. Looking up at Zacchaeus, who had climbed into a sycamore tree in order to see him, Jesus said, 'Make haste and come down, for I must stay at your house to-day'. The impression made upon the taxgatherer, who promised henceforth to restore fourfold to any one he had defrauded, and was called by

[1] I have discussed the saying in detail in *The Gospel according to St. Mark*, 444–6.

Jesus 'a son of Abraham', will always make its appeal as a story which reveals the mind and spirit of the Son of Man who came 'to seek and to save that which was lost' (Lk. xix. 10). It is all the more impressive because it is set at a point so near the arrival of Jesus at Jerusalem.

# XXXVI

# THE CHARACTER OF
# THE JERUSALEM MINISTRY

ITH the arrival of Jesus at Jerusalem we reach a point at which it is impossible to tell the story of his ministry in detail, or even in outline, until we come to the closing scenes. Mark suggests that events moved with great rapidity: from the time of the Entry a week saw the life of Jesus end in the ignominy of the Cross. There are reasons for this representation. By wide consent it is agreed that Mark uses a very early sketch of the Passion Story which originally was compiled for its own sake, in order to meet the needs of worship, instruction, and faith in the Roman community. It is even possible that Mk. xiv–xvi. 8 was preceded by a still briefer account subsequently expanded by the aid of Petrine reminiscences.[1] The structure of Mk. xi–xiii is looser than that of the Passion Narrative proper. The whole is divided into days and the story moves swiftly to its tragic climax. Probably the events described covered a much longer period. Even in Mark there are indications which point to this conclusion. Jesus, it appears, had friends in Jerusalem, as the stories of the preparations made for the Entry and the Last Supper suggest (cf. xi. 2–6, xiv. 13f.), and he taught day by day in the Temple (xiv. 49). In Luke's account this impression is deepened (cf. xix. 47, xxi. 37f.); and it is confirmed by the Fourth Gospel, in which many indica-

[1] This possibility is discussed in my commentary, *The Gospel according to St. Mark*, 653–64.

tions suggest that the Evangelist had access to a valuable source containing much additional information (cf. vii. 10, 14, 32, 37, viii. 20, x. 22, 40–2, xi. 54, xii. 1).

The relationships between the Synoptic and the Johannine accounts are discussed with great learning and insight by M. Goguel in his *Life of Jesus*.[1]  Goguel argues that Jesus left Galilee with his disciples shortly before the Feast of Tabernacles (cf. Jn. vii. 2) in September or October, that he continued to teach in Jerusalem until the Feast of the Dedication (cf. Jn. x. 22) in December, and that soon afterwards he retired across the river Jordan into Peraea (cf. Jn. x. 40, xi. 54).  Thence, he suggests, he returned to the holy city 'six days before the Passover' (Jn. xii. 1) for the final Entry, which led quickly to his arrest and execution.[2]  This hypothesis concerning the course of events depends on our acceptance of the historical statements in the Fourth Gospel, and it is increasingly recognised that we have good reason to accept these statements, in spite of the interpretative element which undoubtedly is to be found in that Gospel.[3]

Within this larger framework we are justified in setting some at least of the five controversy-stories found in Mk. xi. 27–33 and xii. 13–37, especially those connected with the question concerning authority (xi. 27–33) posed by the chief priests, scribes, and elders, the Sadducees' question concerning the resurrection (xii. 18–27), and the counter question of Jesus regarding David's Son (xii. 35–7).  The question of the Pharisees and the Herodians about tribute money (xii. 13–17) and the inquiry of the scribe, 'What commandment is first of all?' (xii. 28–34), may possibly belong to the earlier Galilean

---

[1] Eng. Tr. by Olive Wyon (1933).
[2] *Op. cit.*, 238–50, 401–28.
[3] Cf. C. H. Dodd, *The Interpretation of the Fourth Gospel* (1953).

period. The justification for these suggestions is the probability that Mk. xi. 27–33, xii. 13–37, like Mk. ii. 1–iii. 6, is a pre-Markan compilation constructed originally to illustrate the mortal conflict of Jesus with the Rabbis. As we shall see, some of these stories well indicate the controversies in which Jesus was engaged during the Jerusalem ministry.

With considerable justification Goguel conjectures that the story of the Cleansing of the Temple (Mk. xi. 15–17) may belong to an early stage in this ministry.[1] As is well known, its position varies in the Gospels. In Mark it takes place on the day after the Entry, in Matthew on the day of the Entry itself (xxi. 12–17), and in John on the occasion of the first visit to Jerusalem before the opening of the Galilean ministry proper (ii. 13–22). Its position in the Fourth Gospel seems due to doctrinal considerations, and its Markan setting, in which it breaks the story of the withered fig tree (xi. 12–14, 20–3) into two parts, looks artificial. Goguel attaches great importance to the saying of Jesus regarding the destruction of the Temple, which is embedded in the Johannine narrative (ii. 19), and is echoed in the Markan account of the trial before the priests (xiv. 58) and the story of the Crucifixion (xv. 29). He maintains that it was in consequence of this utterance that Jesus was compelled to withdraw from Jerusalem to Peraea and in the end was condemned to death. Naturally, this suggestion cannot be regarded as more than an interesting and valuable conjecture, but it is certainly in its favour that it throws light upon obscurities and makes possible a credible account of the Jerusalem ministry.

[1] *Op. cit.*, 412–19.

M

# XXXVII

## THE CONTROVERSIES DURING
## THE JERUSALEM MINISTRY

THERE can be no doubt that during his ministry in
Jerusalem Jesus was frequently involved in controversies with the scribes and Pharisees, who sought
to entrap him with dialectical skill. The Markan stories
already mentioned illustrate this device, and the same
testimony is given by the Fourth Gospel. The fact that the
Fourth Evangelist's deepest interests are doctrinal, and
the dramatic form which he gives to the scenes he describes, do not obscure or invalidate the historical basis of
his special tradition. In particular, his account brings
home to the modern reader the ferment of opinion
created by the appearing of the Galilean prophet and his
teaching. Naturally, Messiahship was a primary issue,
and it is clear that on this matter the most various opinions
were held. Some of the descriptive passages in John vii
are especially vivid and lifelike. 'Is not this the man',
said some, 'whom they seek to kill? And here he is,
speaking openly, and they say nothing to him!'. 'Can it
be', they asked, 'that the authorities really know that this
is the Messiah?' (vii. 25f.). Contemporary beliefs are
clearly illustrated when the Jerusalemites object that they
know whence Jesus comes, whereas the Messiah's place
of origin is unknown (Jn. vii. 27), and equally in the
contrary opinion, 'Has not the scripture said that the
Messiah is descended from David, and comes from
Bethlehem, the village where David lived?' (Jn. vii. 41f.).
In another dispute connected with the Feast of the

166

Dedication there is an echo of the reserve with which Jesus treated the question of his Messiahship precisely as he did during the Galilean ministry. Conscious of this reserve, the Jews ask, 'How long will you keep us in suspense? If you are the Messiah, tell us plainly' (Jn. x. 24). In John's account Jesus implicitly accepts the title and appeals to his works as bearing witness to him (Jn. x. 25f.). 'I told you', he says, 'and you believe not'. Only in Jn. iv. 26 does he openly accept the name Christ. Hoskyns[1] rightly points out that this reserve, which is as characteristic of the Fourth Gospel as it is of the Synoptic Gospels, does not mean that he is not the Christ; 'it is occasioned only by the impossibility of setting the Messiahship of Jesus in the context of contemporary Messianic ideas'.

Characteristic of these controversies is the skilful use Jesus makes of the counter-question. When questioned concerning his authority, he asks, 'The baptism of John, was it from heaven, or from men?' (Mk. xi. 30), confronting the hierarchy with a dilemma, which Mark pointedly describes in the words, 'If we shall say, From heaven; he will say, Why then did you not believe him? But shall we say, From men?'[2] Mark breaks off his account of their soliloquy with the deadly statement, 'They feared the people'. Equally notable is the effective use he makes of scripture, as in his question to the Sadducees, 'Have you not read in the book of Moses, in the place concerning the Bush, how God spoke unto him, saying, I am the God of Abraham, and the God of Isaac, and the God of Jacob?' (Mk. xi. 26). Most striking of all is his allusion to Psa. cx. 1,[3] which describes

---

[1] *The Fourth Gospel*, 449.    [2] So RVmg, RSV.

[3] 'The Lord saith unto my lord, Sit thou at my right hand, Until I make thine enemies thy footstool'.

David as 'lord', followed by the challenge, 'David himself calls him Lord; and whence is he his son?' (Mk. xii. 35–7).

The purpose of the question is not to repudiate the idea of the Davidic descent of the Messiah. Still less does it imply that Jesus did not believe himself to be of David's lineage. It suggests rather his conviction that Messiahship is much more than a matter of human descent, but, on the contrary, is supernatural in dignity and origin. This belief is expressed so allusively that it cannot be explained as merely that of the Christian community; it is the conviction of Jesus himself concerning his own person expressed suggestively in his own idiom.[1] We are entitled to infer that, when primitive Christianity confessed him as 'the Son of God', and when the Fourth Evangelist embodies more explicit testimonies to his divine sonship in the Johannine sayings, we are confronted with a legitimate expansion of the tradition which is rooted in the consciousness of Jesus himself. The question, 'Whence is he his son?', is the basis for doctrinal interpretations which pass beyond David to the person of Christ.

The sayings further reveal that Jesus not only engaged in controversy in Jerusalem, but directly attacked the Jewish hierarchy. Mark gives an extract from a sayings-source which shows how severely Jesus arraigned the scribes in the presence of the people. 'Beware of the scribes', he said, and then pointedly referred to their love of walking about in long robes, of salutations in the market places, of the best seats in the synagogues and the chief couches at feasts, to their devouring of widows' houses, and the pretence of their long prayers (Mk. xii. 38–40). Matthew draws upon a fuller account of this

[1] See *The Gospel according to St. Mark*, 490–3.

polemic, from the M source, and shows how Jesus condemned the scribes and Pharisees for their love of titles, their teaching concerning oaths, their scruples about tithes, to the neglect of justice, mercy, and faith, their concern for outward appearances, for the outside of the cup and the platter, in a word, their hypocrisy or 'play-acting' (Mt. xxiii. 1–36, cf. Lk. xi. 39–52).   It has been claimed that this hostility to the scribes is overstated in the Gospels, especially in Matthew.[1]    It may well be that the conditions which existed at the time when the Gospels were written have left their mark on the tradition, and it is true, as the Gospels themselves reveal, that there are signs of more friendly relations between Jesus and the scribes. Mark, for example, tells of a scribe to whom Jesus said, 'You are not far from the kingdom of God' (xii. 34), and Luke shows that sometimes Jesus was invited to dine in the houses of Pharisees (vii. 36, xi. 37, xiv. 1), and was warned by them of the murderous intentions of Herod Antipas (xiii. 31).[2]   Nevertheless, a desire to be fair must not blind us to the fact that, believing sins of the spirit to be more heinous than those of the flesh and that the observance of rules was no substitute for humanity, Jesus rebuked the teachers of the Law in terms of great severity.

The result was inevitable.   John records that the Pharisees on one occasion sent officers to arrest Jesus (vii. 32), and speaks of times when 'the Jews', presumably the rulers, took up stones to stone him (viii. 59, x. 31).   In the closing scenes the hatred of the hierarchy was due,

---

[1] Cf. J. Parkes, *Jesus, Paul and the Jews* (1936), C. G. Montefiore, *The Synoptic Gospels* (2nd ed. 1927).

[2] W. L. Knox, *The Sources of the Synoptic Gospels*, i. 100, suggests that Mt. xxiii. 1 f. may be a survival from a period of Jesus' career 'during which he still hoped that the Pharisees would accept his conception of the kingdom of God'.

not only to the belief that Jesus was a blasphemer, but
also to the memory of occasions when, in the presence of
the people, they had been worsted in the cut and thrust
of argument.  Meantime, during the ministry in Jerusalem, plots to destroy him were thwarted by his marked
popularity with the masses of the people.  All the Gospels
bear witness to this fact.  It can only have been with
popular approval that, in opposition to the vested interests
of the priests, Jesus was able to protest effectively against
the profanation of the Temple by the money changers and
those who sold pigeons in its courts.  'Is it not written',
he cried, 'My house shall be called a house of prayer for
all the nations?  But you have made it a den of robbers'
(Mk. xi. 17).  For the moment they were baffled and could
only wait for an opportunity to destroy Jesus.

# XXXVIII

## THE TEACHING IN JERUSALEM

WHAT was the nature of the teaching given by Jesus during his ministry in Jerusalem and what themes did it include?

One could wish that our sources gave us more explicit information upon these matters, for undoubtedly, if we had it, it would contribute much to our knowledge of his Messianic purpose. As it is, the surviving tradition is mainly controversial. It would be wrong, however, to infer that the Jerusalem ministry was exclusively a period of conflict and controversy. As we have seen, Jesus was frequently involved in disputes about Messiahship, but it may be inferred that this topic was not the main theme of his teaching, but rather an issue which arose out of his ministry. This inference is justified by the fact, previously noted, that he was exhorted to speak plainly and say whether or not he was the Christ (Jn. x. 24). Clearly, upon this subject he maintained the same reserve which had characterised his utterances in Galilee.

In general, we may infer that the main emphasis of his teaching in Jerusalem was laid upon the Kingdom of God, but probably to a greater degree upon its future aspects. He did not renounce the 'realised eschatology' of his earlier ministry, which centred upon the conviction that in himself and his mighty works the Kingdom of God was already present, but was compelled by reason of his teaching concerning Messianic suffering and his perception of the circumstances which would confront his disciples after his death, to dwell upon its consummation.

Proof of this interest is afforded by his sayings at the Last Supper (Mk. xiv. 25, Lk. xxii. 15, 18, 29f.) to which attention will be given later.

The questions to be considered, in the light of the external circumstances of the Jerusalem ministry, are the teaching of Jesus concerning the fate of the city, the eschatological aspects of the Kingdom, and the question of his return or future manifestation to his disciples.

Recent discussions strengthen the conviction that Jesus foresaw, and spoke of, the calamities which would inevitably fall upon Jerusalem.[1] The relevant sayings are more numerous than has commonly been supposed and there is no need to think of them as 'prophecies after the event'. The sayings in Mk. xiii. 15–18 about the man on his housetop and the labourer in the field and the sad situation of women and children depict the horrors of warfare as invading armies swiftly advance. To these sayings there are parallels in Lk. xvii. 31–7. 'On that day', said Jesus, 'let him who is on the housetop, with his goods in the house, not come down to take them away; and let him who is in the field not turn back. Remember Lot's wife'; 'I tell you, in that night there will be two men in one bed: one will be taken and the other left. There will be two women grinding together: one will be taken and the other left'. When he was asked the question, 'Where', he replied enigmatically, 'Where the body is, thither will the vultures also be gathered together'. Especially relevant in this connexion are Lk. xix. 41–4, previously mentioned, Mk. xiii. 14 and Lk. xxi. 20–4.

Closely and inextricably bound up with these prophecies is the eschatological teaching in the discourse of Mk. xiii and, to a less degree, in Lk. xxi. Mk. xiii is the

---

[1] Cf. C. J. Cadoux, *The Historic Mission of Jesus*, 266–79 and C. H. Dodd, *The Journal of Roman Studies*, xxxvii. 47–53.

despair of commentators and Colani's hypothesis of an apocalyptic document, visible mainly in verses 7f., 14–20, 24–7, has for upwards of a century been widely entertained. To-day there is perhaps a growing tendency to recognise in this chapter genuine sayings of Jesus which are seen through an apocalyptic haze. The emphasis in the chapter on premonitory signs is certainly not after his manner and is inconsistent with his explicit statement, 'Of that day, or of that hour, no one knows, not even the angels in heaven, neither the Son, but the Father alone' (Mk. xiii. 32), but it is a rash conclusion to dismiss the eschatological discourse as having nothing to do with his teaching. This opinion is supported by the substantially independent version of the discourse in Lk. xxi. Here Jesus speaks of 'men fainting for fear and with foreboding of what is coming upon the world' (xxi. 26). He bids his disciples lift up their heads because their deliverance is drawing near, to watch at all times, to pray for strength to escape the things that would happen, and to stand before the Son of Man (xxi. 28, 36). Manifestly he foresaw a period of eschatological woes, during which his disciples would be subjected to the threat of persecution. He bade them settle it in their minds not to meditate beforehand when brought before courts of justice, for they would be given 'a mouth and wisdom' which all their adversaries would not be able to gainsay (xxi. 15). Similar teaching appears in the independent oracle on persecution in Mk. xiii. 9–13.

How are we to relate the eschatological teaching of these chapters to the prophecies of impending warfare already mentioned? We are bound, I think, to infer that Jesus did not interpret the immediate future in terms of purely political events. Warfare and persecution in his view were not merely human evils, but manifestations of

Satanic power. Thus he spoke of the investment of Jerusalem in terms of the prophecy of Daniel concerning 'the abomination of desolation' (cf. Dan. ix. 27, xi. 31, xii. 11), which refers to the profanation of the Temple by Antiochus Epiphanes in 168 B.C. Once again Satanic powers would be released, but the triumph of the Son of Man was certain (Mk. xiii. 27f.). These ideas are strange to the modern man, although perhaps less strange to thoughtful minds after the shaking experience of two world wars. As often happens in prophetic forecasts the time of fulfilment is foreshortened and seen in immediate prospect and the language strongly coloured by eschatological imagery and modes of speech.

Did Jesus speak of his own return in power and glory as the Son of Man? Much depends on how we interpret his reply to the high priest during his trial in Mk. xiv. 62, to which consideration will be given later, and on the view we take of the parables which Matthew has connected with the Jerusalem ministry. Many of these parables have been re-interpreted by Matthew and the Church for which he wrote under the strong influence of the apocalyptic hopes of primitive Christianity. We can see this process at work in the interpretation appended to the parable of the Wheat and the Tares (Mt. xiii. 36–43), and in characteristic modifications made by Matthew in his version of the discourse of Mk. xiii (cf. Mt. xxiv. 3, 30f.). It may be doubted, however, whether the attempt to explain such parables as the Thief at Midnight (Mt. xxiv. 43f.), the Waiting Servants (Mt. xxiv. 45–51), the Ten Virgins (Mt. xxv. 1–13), and the Talents (Mt. xxv. 14–30) in terms of 'realised eschatology' is completely successful. The emphasis on the need for watchfulness in many of these parables and in such sayings as Mk. xiii. 33–7 seems to suggest that Matthew has only enhanced an element which is integral to them. He has dotted the 'i's and crossed the 't's of an existing tradition. By this view we account best for the radiant expectation of the Parousia which marked the Church from its beginnings (cf. I. Thess. iv. 13–18, 2 Thess. i. 7f., ii. 1f., Ac. iii. 17–21). In what form Jesus actually spoke of his return, it may be difficult to say, but it is in every way probable that he used colourful Old Testament imagery to express the conviction that the Kingdom would be consummated and that his glory would be manifested to his own. Doubtless, he expected that the interval would be short. And if, in fact, he has indeed returned in the power of his spirit in the life of the Church, this manifestation does not cancel out or foreclose a final revelation of himself in power impossible to picture or date, but none the less assured.

# XXXIX

## TWO PHASES IN
## THE ESCHATOLOGICAL TEACHING

IT may not unjustly be objected that in the account of the ministry of Jesus I have given the teaching concerning the Parousia is duplicated. It is introduced into the early Galilean period and a second time in the last stages of the Jerusalem ministry. It is both 'realised' and 'futuristic' eschatology. Must it not be one thing or the other? Can the question of the Parousia have appeared in different phases of the historic ministry?

This objection has force, especially in the minds of those who favour an attitude of 'either-or' and who tend to think of development as the substitution of truth for error.

In fact, on any scientific estimate of the New Testament evidence, duplication cannot be avoided, for the conditions which bring it about belong to the nature of the tradition. If in the early ministry of Jesus the Son of Man is predominantly the community, it is natural to connect with this teaching sayings and parables relating to the Parousia, however uncertain we may be concerning the date and the relevance of particular utterances. If, on the other hand, the personal use of the name marks the later ministry, the Parousia must again present itself as integral to the teaching. In each case the question of the Parousia of the Son of Man necessarily arises.

This account of the matter, however, unduly simplifies the issue. In reality, the Son of Man is never the community alone and he is never only a person. The two conceptions, the communal and the personal, co-exist, just as the Kingdom is present and future, and precisely as Jesus is the Messiah here and now and *Christus designatus*. Only the atomism of western thought conceals from us the necessary co-existence of these conceptions.

There is an aspect of the place occupied by Jesus in these two phases of teaching which is not unimportant for Christology and is vital to the understanding of the Parousia. So long as the communal aspect is the prominent feature, Jesus is the Son of Man as Head of the Messianic community and as the vicegerent of God. In this phase Parousia sayings, so far as they are relevant, will relate primarily to the community. When, however, the order is reversed, and the personal interpretation of the name is dominant, the Parousia will be that of Jesus himself, the coming of the community being subordinate to his coming. If, then, we are right in thinking that more and more, as his ministry unfolded, Jesus conceived himself to be the Son of Man *par excellence*, he must needs have thought of his Parousia in glory, and all the more since, as the Suffering Son of Man, his suffering is to be subsumed and glorified in victory. Nothing could be more mistaken than to suppose that the application of the Parousia sayings to the community rules out their relevance to Jesus himself, or that their application to Jesus excludes their relevancy for the community. The unfolding we discern in his teaching means that at the end as well as at the beginning the Son of Man must be seen sitting at the right hand of God and coming with the clouds of heaven.

# XL

## THE WITHDRAWAL BEYOND
## THE JORDAN

THE Jerusalem ministry appears to have ended some
time after the Feast of the Dedication in December
(Jn. x. 22). The Fourth Evangelist records that
Jesus 'went away again beyond Jordan into the place
where John was at the first baptizing; and there he
remained' (x. 40). During this period he visited Bethany,
and subsequently 'departed thence into the country near
to the wilderness into a town called Ephraim; and there
he stayed with the disciples' (xi. 54). The Evangelist
tells us nothing of what happened during this withdrawal
except that 'many came to him' and they said, 'John
indeed did no sign: but everything John said about this
man was true' (x. 41). 'Many', he adds, 'believed on
him there' (x. 42). Jesus remained in the wilderness
until the following Passover, a period of three months.
Apparently, he was in almost complete retirement so that
those who remembered him in Jerusalem speculated
whether he would come to the feast (xi. 56). The chief
priests and the Pharisees were unaware of the locality to
which he had gone, and had given orders that if any one
knew where he was, he should let them know, so that
they might arrest him (xi. 57). No doctrinal purpose is
served by the Evangelist's references to this interlude,
and we must conclude that in recording it he was drawing
upon a special tradition unknown to the Synoptists. One
cannot fail to be reminded of the two earlier withdrawals,
to the Judaean wilderness after the baptism before the

Galilean ministry began, and to the borders of Tyre at the close of that ministry. It cannot be accidental nor unimportant that at three crucial moments Jesus deliberately went into retreat.

What was the significance of this third withdrawal? In the complete absence of explicit testimony, we can do no more than relate it to the events which preceded and followed it, the ministry in Jerusalem and the final entry into the city which led to betrayal, crucifixion, and death.

The Jerusalem ministry saw Jesus triumphant over his opponents and in favour with the people. It can only have been because of his popularity that the priests refrained from putting him under arrest while he was in the city, and this is precisely what the Gospels record (cf. Mk. xii. 12, Lk. xix. 47f., Jn. vii. 44). Nevertheless, Jesus can only have interpreted his popularity as failure; it repeated what had already happened in Galilee. His success meant that what he had taught about the kingdom of God, and the warnings he had uttered, were not accepted but interpreted as foolishness. No less than the people of Galilee, the Jerusalemites wanted a Messiah after their own hearts. This is the point of their question when they asked him, 'How long will you keep us in suspense?' and begged him to speak plainly, if he was the Christ (Jn. x. 24). It was this question which told Jesus that he had failed, and this perception which led him to prophesy the destruction of the Temple and the city. It was this situation which drove him across the Jordan. He was again defeated by success.

Goguel[1] describes his departure as a flight. He had claimed that he would destroy the Temple and rebuild it in three days. The claim meant a rupture with Judaism, a

[1] *Op. cit.*, 423.

claim that it had had its day, and it was in consequence of it that Jesus was compelled to seek refuge in Peraea. Then it was, he suggests, that he uttered his lament over Jerusalem which killed the prophets, and declared 'You will not see me until you say, Blessed is he who comes in the name of the Lord' (Mt. xxiii. 37–9, Lk. xiii. 34f.). He hoped, Goguel argues, that on his return the masses would come out boldly for him, and that thus he would be able to brave the opposition of the priests.

It may be that we have done less than justice to this revolutionary saying, which Mark ascribes to false witnesses (xiv. 58), but it is not probable that it is the clue to the departure of Jesus from the city. If he could expect the support of the masses later, he could have counted on it then. He never lost their favour till on his return he destroyed it by his own act. No more than in the case of his withdrawal from Galilee, is it likely that he crossed the Jordan for refuge. He fled, not from his foes, but from his friends. This view is confirmed by the sequel to his subsequent return. After the Entry, as we shall see, there is no more teaching. There was nothing left for him but to die. The explanation that, after leaving Galilee, he came to Jerusalem in the first place to die is incorrect, since, as we have seen, he pursued a vigorous ministry there. Although death lay before him, he had still a task to fulfil in the holy city. But the view that his last visit was a journey to death applies exactly to the situation as it existed then. If these considerations are relevant the significance of his withdrawal beyond the Jordan is apparent. He went there to ponder further the secret of Messianic suffering and death.

We have been too much afraid of reading doctrine into the story of Jesus. We are still too reluctant to do so.

We acquiesce too lightly in the assumption that he went to the cross with no clear idea of what he meant to accomplish.    And yet forty years ago Schweitzer[1] reminded us that there is such a thing as 'dogmatic history', that is, as he says, 'history as moulded by theological beliefs'.    We are too sophisticated to attempt to read back into the thought of Jesus the classical theories of the Atonement, the 'ransom theory' of the early Church, the 'satisfaction theory' of Anselm, the 'moral influence' teaching of Abelard, the 'forensic theories' of the Reformers, although, on reflection, it might occur to us that all these doctrines are not without inner connexion with ideas rooted in the Gospel tradition.    But, even if we are not prepared to admit as much as this, we must cease to cherish the delusion that Jesus faced his cross without the shadow of an idea why he must die and what ends his death would serve. His calm and confident bearing at the betrayal, the arrest, and at the trials before Caiaphas and Pilate is that of one who moves on steadily to his appointed goal.    Although in the garden of Gethsemane he prays that the cup may pass from him, and experiences a sense of desolation on the cross, he is sure that all is of the Father's appointing and that his mission reaches its climax in death and resurrection.

What meditations occupied the mind of Jesus during the months of retirement beyond the Jordan and at Ephraim we have no means of knowing.    If the sayings at the Last Supper give us any clue to his thinking in the closing days of this period, when the events of the Passion lay close at hand, we might surmise that he reflected on such themes as sacrifice, the new covenant, and the final consummation of the Kingdom.    Jesus had his own interpretation of the meaning of Messianic suffering, on

---

[1] *Op. cit.*, 348f.

which he had long reflected. Ephraim was the final crucible of his thinking. He had his own 'doctrine' of the cross, and he shaped it among the stones of the wilderness.

## PART FIVE

## THE PASSION AND RESURRECTION

We come now to the final stage in our account of the life and ministry of Jesus.

For the incidents in this section we are dependent primarily on Mark and L. Matthew follows Mark closely, with additions of a secondary character, and John stands appreciably nearer the Synoptic outline than in any other part of his Gospel. The records suggest that from a very early period the events of the Passion Story were told in the form of a continuous narrative, and there are good reasons for thinking that in outline and in most of the details the account is historically trustworthy. It is true that the first Christians thought of the Passion Story in the light of the Old Testament, and that some of the details are coloured by this interest. This influence, however, has not distorted the records. In some cases the facts have suggested Old Testament passages which give point to what is narrated, without necessarily implying that the accounts are without historical foundation. Throughout the note of wonder pervades the Story. In contrast with the apocryphal Passion Gospels, it is especially noteworthy how rarely Jesus speaks. The first narrators felt that it was enough to relate the events, without commenting upon them, and without making Jesus the mouthpiece of their doctrinal views. The result is that the reader is himself brought near to the events as they happened.

# XLI

## THE FINAL ENTRY INTO JERUSALEM

A FEW days before the Passover Jesus made a significant entry into Jerusalem. On the basis of the later accounts in Matthew and in John the incident is often described as the Triumphal Entry, but this name is misleading as a careful study of Mark and Luke shows. The incident undoubtedly has a Messianic character, but it is not so much an attempt to claim Messiahship as a last endeavour on the part of Jesus to correct the Messianic expectations of his followers and to bring home to them the nature of Messiahship as he himself understood it.

In Matthew's account (xxi. 1–17) Jesus is hailed as 'the Son of David'. The whole city is stirred. The people of Jerusalem ask, 'Who is this?' and receive the reply, 'This is the prophet Jesus from Nazareth of Galilee', an answer somewhat in contrast with the Matthaean narrative as a whole. The blind and the lame are healed in the Temple; the children cry, 'Hosanna to the Son of David', and Jesus is said to answer the protests of the priests by saying, 'Yes: have you never read, Out of the mouths of babes and sucklings thou hast perfected praise?' (xxi. 16, cf. Psa. viii. 2). John also depicts a regal figure, who is greeted with palm branches and acclaimed as 'the King of Israel'. Both Evangelists quote the prophecy of Zech. ix. 9, which describes a king, not in the form of a warrior on horseback, but as one speaking peace to the nations, meek, and riding upon an ass (Mt. xxi. 5, Jn. xii. 15). Manifestly, these accounts embellish the story, and for a

truer version of the events we must consult the narratives
of Mark and Luke.

Although Mark does not quote Zech. ix. 9, the prophecy is implied by his story, and the inference is justified
that, inspired by it, Jesus determined to enter Jerusalem
in a manner which in itself would dramatize his spiritual
conception of Messiahship.    Teaching had failed;
would prophetic action be more potent?    By previous
arrangement, he despatched two of his disciples to
Bethany, where they found a colt tied at the door in the
open street.    Bringing it to Jesus, the disciples threw
their garments over it, and set him thereon.    So in
humble guise, and yet to the discerning eye as king, he
approached Jerusalem.    Many spread their clothes on the
road, and others scattered leafy sprays which they had
gathered from the fields.    Nevertheless, the people were
puzzled.    There is a curious restraint in their acclama-
tions, which stop just short of a Messianic ovation.
'Hosanna!', they cry, 'Blessed be he who comes in the
name of the Lord!    Blessed be the kingdom of our father
David that is coming!    Hosannah in the highest!' (Mark
xi. 9f.).    The cry invokes God for aid and blessing.
Already, it would seem, the situation was growing
dangerous with incipient Messianic excitement.    Luke
records that some of the Pharisees urged Jesus to rebuke
his disciples, but he replied, 'I tell you that if these were
silent, the very stones would cry out' (Lk. xix. 40).    It is
usual to interpret this reply as a defence of the disciples,
but I am inclined to think that for once Jesus agreed with
the Pharisees.    His reply is a cry of anguish.    He feels
that nothing he can say, and nothing he can do, is of any
avail to dispel the atmosphere of political Messianism.
The very stones are impregnated with it!    He knew that
his final bid had failed!    It is in harmony with this view

that, when the white pinnacles of the city came in sight, he wept over it. 'If thou hadst known in this day, even thou, the things which belong unto peace! but now they are hid from thine eyes!' (Lk. xix. 42).

The incident breaks off and, so far as we can see, passed unnoticed in Jerusalem at large. No reference to it is made in the trial scenes, as might well have been the case if it had been a triumphal entry. Perhaps he had known that his intention would fail, but had felt that no effort must be spared to wean his followers from futile hopes. In contrast with the later Evangelists, Mark relates that he entered into the Temple, looked round upon all and then departed, since it was late afternoon, for Bethany with the Twelve (Mk. xi. 11). A chill must have fallen upon the hearts of all his friends as they climbed the heights of the Mount of Olives. They remained with him, perhaps hoping against hope, for there was nothing else they could do. But Judas, one of the Twelve, more astute than the rest, understood. The farce, as it seemed to him, had ended! Jesus had no intention of being a political Messiah and of calling the people to his standard! What must he do?

Meantime, Jesus bivouacked on the Mount of Olives (Lk. xxi. 37). Only too clearly he saw that the issue was death. When later the woman at Bethany broke the alabaster jar of ointment over his head, he said, 'She has done what she could; she has anointed my body before-hand for burying' (Mk. xiv. 8).

# XLII

## THE BETRAYAL

THE betrayal of Jesus by a chosen disciple, 'one of the Twelve', has all the pathos of a Greek tragedy. The first Christians were stunned and astounded by the deed. Mark re-iterates the phrase just used (xiv. 10, 20, 43). Influenced by Zech. xi. 12, Matthew says that his price was thirty pieces of silver (xxvi. 15). Luke attributes his action to Satan (xxii. 3) and John does the same (xiii. 27). John also charges him with habitual theft (xii. 6) and describes his departure from the Supper with dramatic irony: 'So, after receiving the morsel, he immediately went out; and it was night' (xiii. 30). It is greatly to the credit of the Evangelists that they do not conceal, or gloss over, his traitorous deed.

Modern attempts to excuse Judas' act are vain, yet it is not beyond understanding. A hope that by his action Jesus might be forced to assert his Messianic claims has been charitably suggested as a motive for the crime, but it is much more likely that he was driven to act by disillusionment and despair. He read the secret of Jesus better than anyone else, but missed its glory, blinded by despair. With the insight of perfect goodness Jesus read his mind. At the Supper he said, 'Alas for that man by whom the Son of Man is delivered up! It would have been better for that man if he had not been born' (Mk. xiv. 21). These words are not a threat, but an expression of the deepest sadness. At the arrest, as a last appeal to a darkened heart, he gave to him the old familiar greeting, 'Friend, why are you here?' (Mt. xxvi. 50), a mode of

address which Deissmann[1] has shown was familiar in the
first century A.D.  The words did not dissuade him from
completing his deed, but it is permissible to suppose that
they made a deep impression.  Matthew's statement that
subsequently he threw down the silver in the Temple and
cried, 'I have sinned in betraying innocent blood'
(xxvii. 4), reflects popular tradition, but is a telling
dramatic picture of his repentance.  Legend speaks of his
frightful end.  According to Mt. xxvii. 5, he 'went away
and hanged himself'.  Ac. i. 18 says that 'falling head-
long, he burst asunder in the midst'.  Certainty is no
longer attainable, speculation has proved common.  The
most plausible speculation is that it was the love of Jesus
that convicted and slew him.

What was it that Judas betrayed?  The well known
answer of Schweitzer[2] is that he betrayed the Messianic
secret of Jesus.  This explanation ought not lightly to be
rejected.  The priests had long wanted to arrest Jesus as a
Messianic pretender dangerous to peace, but they lacked
convincing evidence, as the incriminating question of
Caiaphas at the trial shows.  There can be little doubt
that they would have jumped at the opportunity to call
Judas as a witness for the prosecution.  This explanation,
however, does not rule out the older answer, that Judas
betrayed the secret of the place where Jesus might be
apprehended.  It is true that spies might have secured
this information, but it was a great advantage to the hierarchy that no such steps were necessary.  In the greatest
secrecy, as they desired (cf. Mk. xiv. 2), guided by a
disciple, they could effect the arrest of Jesus.  And this
they did.

[1] Cf. *Light from the Ancient East*, 125–31.
[2] Cf. *The Quest of the Historical Jesus*, 394.

# XLIII

## THE LAST SUPPER

LIKE the final entry into Jerusalem, the Last Supper appears to have been celebrated with deliberation and intention. As at Bethany, so in Jerusalem Jesus had made arrangements for the feast with a householder, for it was necessary to eat the Passover meal in the city. 'Go into the city', he said to two of his disciples, 'and a man carrying a jar of water will meet you; follow him, and wherever he enters, say to the householder, The teacher says, Where is my guest room, where I am to eat the Passover with my disciples?' (Mk. xiv. 14). We may, if we will, attribute this command to prophetic foresight, but it seems more probable that Jesus had an understanding with a friend on whom he could rely. From the instructions given it is clear that the meal in prospect was the feast of the Passover, and since Mark goes on to describe the meal, we must infer that the Evangelist identified it with the Passover, in the belief that the intention of Jesus was fulfilled. Several features, however, in Mark are inconsistent with this representation. No lamb is mentioned and there is no reference to bitter herbs regularly eaten at the Passover meal. Moreover, later in the evening some of the disciples and the men who effected the arrest were carrying arms. More important still, according to the Fourth Gospel the Passover had not yet been celebrated at the time of the trial before Pilate. The Jews, we are told, 'did not enter the praetorium, that they might not be defiled, but might eat the Passover' (Jn. xviii. 28, cf. xix. 14). There is thus a difference

190

between Mark and John in respect of the date.   Attempts
to reconcile the two Gospels are not convincing, and,
accordingly, it is necessary to decide between them.   On
this issue critical opinion is widely divided.   Recently
strong arguments have been put forward in favour of the
Markan date,[1] but the Johannine date seems to me to be
preferable,[2] supported as it is by indirect evidence in
Mark and Luke,[3] and especially by the fact that the priests
wished to avoid an arrest during the feast (Mk. xiv. 2).
If the Johannine date is accepted, we must infer that,
owing to the swift march of events, Jesus celebrated the
meal twenty-four hours earlier than he had intended.
Even in this case Paschal ideas must have been dominant
in his mind.

The Supper was no ordinary meal.   Irresistibly, it
recalls the fellowship meal in the wilderness (Mk. vi.
35–44), when at the bidding of Jesus the disciples and the
multitude ate bread and fish in anticipation of the Messianic Feast.   The same verbs are used: 'He took bread,
and blessed, and broke it, and gave to them' (Mk. xiv.
22, cf. vi. 41) and, with reference to the wine, he said,
'Truly I tell you, I shall not drink again of the fruit of the
vine until that day when I drink it new in the kingdom of
God' (Mk. xiv. 25, cf. Lk. xxii. 16).   The Supper, then,
looked forward; it was an eschatological sacrament which
anticipated the coming of the Kingdom of God.   The
eating of bread and the sharing of the cup were more than
symbolic actions; they were effective symbols pledging
the disciples to a share in the life of the consummated

---

[1] Cf. Dalman, *Jesus Jeshua*, 86–184; Jeremias, *Die Abendmahlsworte Jesu*,[2] 18–46, *JTS*, l. 1–10; A. J. B. Higgins, *The Lord's Supper in the New Testament*, 13–23

[2] *The Gospel according to St. Mark*, 664–7.

[3] Cf. Lk. xxii. 15, which, as Burkitt and Brooke suggest, seems to express an unfulfilled desire.

Kingdom. But this is not all, for thus far the Supper does not differ in substance from the fellowship-meal, or meals, in Galilee. The Last Supper has a distinctive character intentionally imposed upon it by Jesus himself in view of his impending death. Taking the bread, he broke it and said, 'Take; this is my body'. By these words he gave the bread a totally new significance, a change, in fact, of values. In virtue of his command the act of eating was to be a spiritual means whereby they might share in the power of his approaching sacrifice.

This significance of the Supper is even more explicit in the words spoken at the giving of the cup. 'This', Jesus said, 'is my blood of the covenant, which is poured out for many' (Mk. xiv. 24, cf. I Cor. xi. 25). 'They all drank of it', Mark writes, and the narrative suggests that their action was meant to be a pledge of sharing in a new covenant, which Jesus was establishing, just as surely as the Israelites were given a share in the covenant of Sinai, when Moses took blood and sprinkled it upon them.[1] It is not to be supposed that the Twelve understood at the time all that Jesus meant. It is, indeed, characteristic of him that he did not always aim at being immediately understood. It is not plausible to trace the origin of the story to Greek ideas and practices. The Old Testament and the creative mind of Jesus supply all that is necessary to account for its ideas and sayings.

Important as the story is in its bearing upon the supreme rite of Christian worship, it is also significant to the historian as providing a window through which can be seen something of the mind of Jesus as he faced rejection and death. Manifestly, he did not think of his death

---

[1] Cf. R. Otto, *The Kingdom of God and the Son of Man*, 265–311; J. Jeremias, *op. cit.*, 107; V. Taylor, *Jesus and His Sacrifice*, 114–42, *The Gospel according to St. Mark*, 545f.

merely as a judicial murder or a physical tragedy. He believed it to be the divinely appointed means whereby a new covenant relationship would be established between God and men. He would suffer as the Son of Man, the head of the new Messianic community, which it was his Father's will to establish. His life, like that of the Servant of the Lord, would be poured out for many who by his stripes would be healed.

In this confidence he conversed with his disciples after the Supper in words preserved by Luke in Lk. xxii. 24–38, by Mark in his account of the journey to Gethsemane (xiv. 26–31), and, spiritually interpreted, by the Fourth Evangelist in the sublime meditation of Jn. xiv–xvii. He foresaw the approaching defection of Peter and prophesied that he would deny him before the morning. He contrasted the present situation of the disciples, exposed as they would be to many perils, with their position when in Galilee they went out on their mission 'without purse, and wallet, and shoes' and, on their own admission, lacked nothing (Lk. xxii. 35). 'But now', he said, speaking in colourful speech, 'he who has a purse, let him take it, and likewise a wallet: and he who has none, let him sell his mantle, and buy a sword'. Things were going to be very different, for the prophecy of Isaiah, 'And he was reckoned with transgressors', was about to be fulfilled in himself. So dull were they of understanding, that when, taking his words literally, they replied, 'Lord, here are two swords', he could only say sadly, 'It is enough' (Lk. xxii. 38). We cannot recover the exact form of the tradition which the Fourth Evangelist develops in his Supper-discourses, but it is clear that he is true to the historical situation when he writes: 'Behold, the hour cometh, yea, is come, that you shall be scattered, every man to his own, and shall leave me alone:

and yet I am not alone, because the Father is with me'
(Jn. xvi. 32). One inevitably recalls the different, but
similar, Markan passage, 'All you will be made to stumble:
for it is written, I will smite the shepherd, and the sheep
will be scattered' (Mk. xiv. 27). The Johannine account
ends with the triumphant words, 'These things have I
spoken to you, that in me you may have peace. In the
world you have tribulation: but be of good cheer; I have
overcome the world' (Jn. xvi. 33). Mark ends the story
of the upper room with the statement that they sang a
hymn, perhaps the second part of the Hallel, Psalms
cxv–cxviii, and that 'they went out to the Mount of
Olives' (Mk. xiv. 26).

# XLIV

# GETHSEMANE

ROM the upper room Jesus with his disciples withdrew to a place called 'Gethsemane', literally 'oils-
press'. Apparently, it was a former farmstead or
country estate planted with olive trees at the foot, or on
the lower slopes, of the Mount of Olives. Arriving there,
Jesus said to his disciples, 'Sit here, while I pray' (Mk.
xiv. 32), and taking with him Peter, James, and John, he
went further into the garden. In Mark's poignant words
he 'began to be greatly distressed and troubled'. 'My
soul', he said to them, 'is exceeding sorrowful even unto
death: abide here and watch'. Going forward a little, he
prayed, 'Abba, Father, all things are possible unto thee;
remove this cup from me: howbeit not what I will, but
what thou wilt'. According to a very early and independent account in Lk. xxii. 43f.,[1] he was divinely
strengthened, and, being in an agony, prayed the more
earnestly, while his sweat 'became as it were great drops of
blood falling down upon the ground'. Manifestly, the
calm of the upper room had gone, replaced by a state of
great mental anguish coupled with a human hope that in
some way the destiny of death might even yet be averted,
but no less with a confident acceptance of the Father's
will. The Gospels do not attempt to explain his agony
and no one can explain it fully. We can at least be sure
that his anguish was not only the fear of death, nor is any

---

[1] For the textual problems see Streeter, *The Four Gospels*, 137f., and
C. S. C. Williams, *Alterations to the Text of the Synoptic Gospels and Acts*,
6–8. See also W. L. Knox, *The Sources of the Synoptic Gospels*, i. 127.

theological necessity imposed upon us of explaining it as
punishment inflicted upon him for the sins of men. A
connexion, however, with the fact of human sin is
inescapable, and for my own part I do not think we can
describe his suffering otherwise than as an experience of
'sin-bearing'. Two considerations support this view.
To share in the consequences of sin is the lot of all who
love men greatly, and to a unique degree this experience
must have been that of Jesus as he saw the hypocrisy of
the scribes, the pride of the priests, the materialism of the
masses, the blindness of the disciples, and the treachery of
Judas. Further, 'sin-bearing' was necessarily involved in
the communal aspects of his person and of his ministry as
he interpreted it. Even the prophet Jeremiah had said,
'For the hurt of the daughter of my people am I hurt'
(Jer. viii. 21), and of the Servant it was said, 'he bore the
sin of many' (Isa. liii. 12). As the Son of Man and the
Servant of the Lord he must needs have felt the sins of
Israel as a burden which it was his mission to carry, and
from which therefore he could not escape. We have no
saying expressly to this effect, although it must be held to
be implied in the prophecies of the Passion as a whole.
The clearest is the allusion to Isa. liii. 12 in Lk. xxii.
37, a passage already mentioned[1], in which the words, 'And
he was reckoned with transgressors', are quoted, especially if we may render the words which follow, 'for my
life draws to its end'.[2] Even if the saying is Christian
interpretation, it may be held to be valid interpretation
which 'brings out' what is implied elsewhere. 'Sin-
bearing' indeed may be held to be an ingredient of
the cup of which he spoke to James and John (Mk. x.

[1] See p. 142f.
[2] So Klostermann, Luce, *in loc.*, Swete, *Studies in the Teaching of our Lord*, 111.

38f.), 'the cup that I drink', and which now for a moment he asks to be taken away from him (Mk. xiv. 36). The use of the symbol of the cup in the Old Testament[1] suggests that Jesus is speaking of intense spiritual suffering.

The suffering was all the greater because it was unshared. One must suppose that Peter, James, and John were separated from the rest of the disciples in order that they might have some part in the Messianic suffering of Jesus. The possibility of a conflict with daemonic powers is suggested by the exhortation, 'Watch and pray, that you may not enter into temptation' (Mk. xiv. 38, Lk. xxii. 40).[2] As it was, the chosen three were asleep. Deep sorrow sounds in the reproach of Jesus, 'Simon, are you asleep? Could you not watch one hour?'. Schematisation has been seen in the threefold return of Jesus,[3] but there is much point in the comment of J. Weiss, 'The irresistible lethargy of the disciples was for Peter a shameful memory'.[4] The final words have the deepest pathos if they are rendered, 'Still asleep? Still resting? The end is far away? The hour has come' (Mk. xiv. 41). The reference to 'the hour' is characteristic of the thought of Jesus.[5] Eschatological in origin, it suggests the thought of conflict in the fulfilment of his Messianic destiny. It is significant that, even after their defection, Jesus associates the three disciples with him in the command, 'Arise, let us be going. Behold, he who delivers me up is near'.

---

[1] Cf. Psa. lxxv. 8, Isa. li. 17–23, Jer. xlix. 12, Lam. iv. 21, Ezek. xxiii. 31–4.

[2] Cf. Apoc. iii. 10.

[3] W. L. Knox, *op. cit.*, 128, suggests the use of different sources.

[4] *Das älteste Evangelium*, 301.

[5] Cf. xiv. 35 and i. 15, xiii. 32.

# XLV

## THE ARREST

THE arrest was made by a company, armed with swords and clubs, sent by the chief priests and led by Judas (Mk. xiv. 43). John says that a cohort of Roman soldiers was present (xviii. 3), and if there was collusion[1] between the priests and Pilate, the presence of at least a detachment is probable. Judas had already arranged a token by which Jesus might be recognised in the darkness, and coming to him he cried, 'Rabbi', and kissed him. The reference to the arrest is given by Mark in the barest possible words, 'And they laid hands on him, and took him' (Mk. xiv. 46). So the story appears to have been told in the oldest Roman community. To it the Evangelist adds a few details from his special tradition, the reference to an unnamed disciple who drew his sword and cut off the ear of the high priest's servant, the reproach of Jesus, 'Have you come out as against a robber?', the statement that all the disciples forsook him and fled, and an allusion to a young man, either Mark himself or more probably an informant, who followed and only escaped arrest by leaving the linen cloth with which he was clothed in the hands of the crowd. From Gethsemane Jesus was led away to the high priest's house, where members of the Jewish hierarchy foregathered. In Mark the account of a trial by night follows, but with greater probability[2] Luke places the trial early on the following morning. The origin of the confusion is probably the

[1] Cf. M. Goguel, *The Life of Jesus*, 468.
[2] So F. C. Burkitt, *The Gospel History and its Transmission*, 136.

fact that a private examination took place in the house of
Annas, the father-in-law of Caiaphas, before Jesus was
sent to the high priest (Jn. xviii, 12, 19, 24). Meantime
Jesus was mocked by his captors and denied by Peter.

fact that a private examination took place in the house of
Annas, the father-in-law of Caiaphas, before Jesus was
sent to the high priest (Jn. xviii. 12, 19, 24). Meantime
Jesus was mocked by his captors and denied by Peter.

# XLVI

## THE MOCKING

IN Mark, in consequence of the time to which he has
assigned the trial, the identity of those who mocked
Jesus is obscure. Luke's account, which assigns this
act to 'the men who held' Jesus, presumably those who
had effected the arrest, is inherently more probable (Lk.
xxii. 63). In this account Jesus is blindfolded, and the
mockers say, 'Prophesy: who is he that struck you?'.
In the usually accepted text of Mark, reference is also
made to the covering of the face of Jesus and to buffeting,
but here the injunction, 'Prophesy', has less meaning.
There is much justice therefore in the suggestion of
Turner[1] and Streeter,[2] which is supported by important
textual evidence, that the reference to the covering of the
face in Mark is an assimilation to the text of Luke, and that
originally Mark wrote, 'And some began to spit upon his
face, and to buffet him, and to say to him, Prophesy'.
'In Mark', writes Streeter, 'the mockers spit on His face
and slap Him and cry, "Play the prophet now". In Luke
they veil His eyes and then, striking Him, say, "Use
your prophetic gift of second sight to tell the striker's
name". Each version paints a consistent picture'.[3] This
suggestion is attractive, but the textual question, as is so
often the case, is still a matter for discussion, and, even if
the two versions are different, it by no means follows that
we must choose one and reject the other. The mocking
need not have been a single incident, and in spite of the

---

[1] *JTS*, xxix, 10*f*.        [2] *The Four Gospels*, 325–8.
[3] *Op. cit.*, 327.

danger of adopting a harmonising expedient, it must be
allowed that Jesus can have been satirically urged to play
the prophet and also, while blindfolded, have been subjected to a vulgar test.  The closing statement in Mark
concerning the attendants who 'received him with blows'
may reflect the influence of Isa. l. 6, 'I gave . . . my cheeks
unto blows', but there is no reason to think that this influence goes deep or is responsible for the genesis of the
story.  There are too many instances in history of in-
dignities heaped upon innocent prisoners to render such
an explanation necessary.

# XLVII

## THE DENIAL

M EANTIME, within sight of his Master, Peter
denied that he was a follower of the Nazarene.
He had followed the crowd from afar, but had
gone right inside the court of the high priest's house, and
was sitting with the attendants and warming himself in the
light of a fire. When challenged by a maidservant, he
replied, 'I neither know him, nor have I any idea what you
can mean'[1] (Mk. xiv. 68), and he repeated his denial when
he went out into the forecourt. When still later the
bystanders repeated the charge, and commented upon his
Galilean speech, he began to call down the wrath of God
upon himself, if what he said was not true. ' I don't know
this man of whom you speak', he said. Mark twice draws
attention to the crowing of a cock and records that Peter
remembered the prophecy of Jesus, and that bursting into
tears he began to weep. Montefiore[2] rightly says that the
whole scene is 'indelibly fixed in the consciousness of the
Western world', and recalls the opinion of Loisy, that 'if
there is an actual reminiscence from Peter anywhere in the
second Gospel it is most certainly in the story of the
denial in the form in which it is found in Mark'. With a
sense of the dramatic Luke says that 'the Lord turned and
looked upon Peter', and suggests that it was then that he
remembered the words of Jesus (Lk. xxii. 61). With the
Synoptic story that of John is in substantial agreement,
but with variations in detail, adding that it was through

---

[1] So C. H. Turner, *The Gospel according to St. Mark*, 74.
[2] *The Synoptic Gospels*, i. 368.

the influence of another disciple 'known unto the high priest' that Peter gained admission to the courtyard (Jn. xviii. 16).

## XLVIII

## THE TRIAL BEFORE CAIAPHAS

THE trial scenes are not accounts of trials in the strict sense of the term, since it is clear that the chief priests had already decided upon their course of action and wished to give it a show of legality. In agreement with Luke's account I have already accepted the view that the examination before Caiaphas, as distinct from a preliminary inquiry the night before, was held in the early morning, but Mark's narrative gives a reliable version of what took place. The anxiety of the priests was to secure testimony which would sustain a charge of blasphemy based upon the saying of Jesus, 'I will destroy this temple (that is made with hands), and in three days I will build another (not made with hands)' (Mk. xiv. 58). Mark takes the view that the charge was false and that the testimony of the witnesses did not agree. Later, however, he records that the taunt was made during the Crucifixion, 'Aha! You who would destroy the temple and build it in three days, save yourself, and come down from the cross' (Mk. xv. 29). There can be no doubt that this saying of Jesus gave great offence, for it embodied the tacit Messianic claim that he would establish the new Temple as was expected in contemporary apocalyptic beliefs,[1] but which he interpreted spiritually of the new Messianic community. Mark's account of this saying and the form it assumes in Mt. xxvi. 61[2] may reflect a certain uneasiness on the part of the Jerusalem disciples who continued to

---

[1] Cf. I Enoch xc. 29, 4 Ezra ix. 38–x. 27, and the Targum on Isa. liii. 5.
[2] 'This man said, I am able to destroy the temple of God ...'.

observe the practice of Temple worship.[1] In any case the priests were baffled because Jesus refused to answer the question whether the testimony was true. Then it was that Caiaphas put the direct challenge, 'Are you the Messiah, the Son of the Blessed?'. In Matthew and in Luke this question is answered in the affirmative, but in a way which indicates a difference of interpretation between Jesus and the priests. In Mt. xxvi. 64 the answer appears in the form, 'You have said so', and in Lk. xxii. 70 in the words, 'You say that I am'. In the accepted text of Mark the direct affirmative answer appears, 'I am' (xiv. 62), but in important manuscripts it has the form, 'You said that I am', and it is not improbable that this is the answer that was given. If so, the answer was not an evasion, nor even a hesitating reply, but it threw the onus on Caiaphas, as if to say, 'The word is yours', 'Yes, if you like', thus indicating that Jesus understood Messiahship in his own way. This representation is entirely in line with the 'Messianic secret' of Jesus so frequently suggested in Mark. No answer could show more clearly how much Jesus disliked the title 'the Messiah', not because he rejected the office, but because his view of its nature and that of his generation were poles asunder.

After this reply Jesus went on to speak of the session of the Son of Man on high and his coming in glory: 'You will see the Son of Man sitting at the right hand of power, and coming with the clouds of heaven' (Mk. xiv. 62). The name 'Power', or 'the Power' was a contemporary way of speaking of God, and the saying embodies allusions to Psa. cx. 1 and to Dan. vii. 13. Matthew says that the session on high will be seen 'hereafter' by the priests (xxvi. 64). Luke describes it as a state which will

---

[1] Cf. Ac. ii. 46, iii. 1–10, v. 20f., 42.

exist 'from now', but omits the reference to the clouds (xxii. 69). Probably Mark's version is the more original form of the saying. In view of Mk. viii. 38 and xiii. 26 it is probable that the Evangelist understood the words to refer to Christ's Parousia. If so, they were not fulfilled in the lifetime of the priests, and the whole problem of the delay of the Parousia is before us. It is probable, however, that Jesus was speaking of much more than a spectacular return to earth. The vital statement in Psa. cx. 1 is 'The Lord said unto my lord, Sit thou at my right hand', and in Dan. vii. 13, 'There came with the clouds of heaven one like unto a son of man'. It may well be that in speaking of things which the priests would see, Jesus was thinking of his own acknowledgement as the Son by his Father and the establishing of the Elect community, with himself as its Head, in the earth, of a visible triumph so difficult to imagine in the circumstances in which he stood before the council. The advantage of this interpretation is that, if it is valid, it explains why the high priest tore his garments and cried 'Blasphemy!' It was not blasphemy to claim to be the Messiah, but to speak with assurance of sharing the throne of God and of the fulfilment of Daniel's vision in himself and his community was blasphemy indeed. No wonder Caiaphas cried, 'Why do we still need witnesses? You have heard the blasphemy!' In reply to his question, 'What do you think?', Mark writes, 'And they all condemned him as deserving of death' (Mk. xiv. 64).

It is still a disputed question how far at this period the Sanhedrin possessed the power to pass capital sentences.[1] The implication of the Gospel narratives is that this right belonged solely to the Roman procurator, and the historian Mommsen says that in essentials Mark's

---

[1] Cf. G. D. Kilpatrick, *The Trial of Jesus* (1953).

account is accurate.  He states that, after a consultation, Jesus was bound, and carried away, and delivered up to Pilate.  He alone, it is implied, could decide and carry out the sentence of death.

# XLIX

# THE TRIAL BEFORE PILATE

ONTIUS PILATE was procurator of Judaea from A.D. 25/26 to 36 under the imperial *legatus* of Syria. Josephus[1] describes his cruelty and oppression, and Philo[2] quotes a letter from Agrippa I to the emperor Caligula which speaks of him as 'inflexible, merciless, and obstinate' and gives a terrible catalogue of his crimes and excesses. Scholars debate whether he determined to destroy Jesus on cynical grounds of policy, and whether his repeated declarations in the Gospels that he had found no crime in Jesus (Lk. xxiii. 4, 14, 22) merely reflect an apologetic motive on the part of the Evangelists. The descriptions of Pilate mentioned above, and the reference in Lk. xiii. 1 to the Galileans whose blood he had mingled with their sacrifices, favour the more sinister opinion, but all our sources mention his vacillation, although some of them to the point of over-emphasis (cf. Mt. xxvii. 24–6, Jn. xix. 12). Probably he was astute enough to see through the pretentions of the priests and to recognise the innocence of Jesus, but not strong enough to stake all upon a bold decision.

Mark's account implies that the priests charged Jesus with pretending to be 'the king of the Jews' (xv. 2), and Luke's special source states the political accusation even more fully: 'We found this man perverting our nation, and forbidding us to give tribute to Caesar, and saying that he himself is Christ a king' (Lk. xxiii. 2). This was a

[1] *Antiquities*, xviii. 2. 2., 3. 1f., 4. 1f.  *Bellum Jud.* ii. 9. 2–4.
[2] *Leg. ad Gaium*, 38.

charge which Pilate could not dismiss lightly, even if he
had wished to do so. He was bound therefore to ask the
decisive question, 'Are *you* the king of the Jews?', but the
stress laid on the pronoun indicates an attitude of dis-
belief and contempt. To this question Jesus answered in
the same enigmatic manner in which he had replied to
Caiaphas, 'You have said so'. When the chief priests
pressed their accusations, he asked Jesus, 'Have you no
answer? See how many accusations they bring against
you', but to his astonishment the prisoner made no further
reply. The Fourth Evangelist has given a highly
dramatic account of this incident, which enables him to
give a spiritual interpretation of Christ's true kingship
(Jn. xviii. 33–8) and to dwell upon the political aspects of
the trial and the issue Caesar or Christ (Jn. xix. 12–16).
Mark's account is impressive by its brevity and restraint;
no attempt is made to raise later religious issues. To
relate the stark facts was felt to be enough.

At this point Mark mentions that at the feast the
governor was wont to release a prisoner at the request of
the people, and explains that a certain Barabbas was lying
bound along with revolutionists who had committed
murder. This custom is not otherwise attested, but
ancient analogies have been cited.[1] For the first time in
his narrative the Evangelist mentions the crowd who
'came up' and asked that the custom might be observed.
The fact that the crowd comes up for this purpose, and
apparently not to witness the trial of Jesus,[2] adds veri-
similitude to the story. Taking advantage of their
presence Pilate asked if they would like him to release
to them the king of the Jews, and, with one of his rare
comments, Mark observes that 'he perceived that for envy

[1] Cf. V. Taylor, *The Gospel according to St. Mark*, 580f.
[2] So Ed. Meyer, *Ursprung und Anfänge des Christentums*, i. 195.

the chief priests had delivered him up' (xv. 10). Stirred up by the priests, the people asked rather for Barabbas, and when Pilate asked what then he should do to him whom they called 'the king of the Jews', they cried 'Crucify him'. Without avail Pilate asked, 'Why, what evil has he done?', only to provoke further the cry, 'Crucify him'. This choice, depicted by John in the form, 'Not this man, but Barabbas' (xviii. 40), has left a deep impression in the earliest tradition. It is doubly dramatic, since, by the irony of history, the rebel's name was 'Jesus Barabbas', as the Caesarean text of Mt. xxvii. 16f. attests, and modern scholars affirm.[1]

The astonishing change in the crowd, from hanging upon the words of Jesus during the Jerusalem ministry (Lk. xix. 48) to 'Crucify him', is due only in part to the traditional fickleness of crowds. As Mark relates, they were incited to action by the priests (xv. 11), and doubtless enraged at the fear of being robbed of the release of Barabbas. Most of all they must have been deeply disappointed by the passivity and the silence of Jesus. Like Judas, they saw that he had no intention of becoming a national leader. There is no rage like that of a crowd deceived by its dearest expectations, no idol that it will not throw down when enthusiasm gives place to contempt. That is why the people cried, 'Away with him', 'Crucify him'.

In this amazing story, in which drama appears at every point, the action of Pilate is described with astonishing restraint: 'And Pilate, wishing to content the multitude, released unto them Barabbas, and delivered Jesus, when he had scourged him, to be crucified' (Mk. xv. 15).

---

[1] So Burkitt, McNeile, Streeter, Rawlinson, Deissmann, and others. Cf. C.S.C. Williams, *Alterations to the Text of the Synoptic Gospels and Acts*, 31–3.

Luke writes: 'And their voices prevailed. . . . He released the man who had been thrown into prison for insurrection and murder, whom they asked for: but Jesus he delivered up to their will' (xxiii. 23–5).

Luke writes: 'And their voices prevailed. . . . He released
the man who had been thrown into prison for insurrection
and murder, whom they asked for: but Jesus he delivered up to their will' (xxiii. 23-5).

L

# THE CRUCIFIXION

THE outstanding characteristic of the Crucifixion
narratives is their realism. The dreadful facts are
faithfully reported, but no attempt is made to
dwell upon the details of what Cicero has described as 'the
most cruel and hideous of punishments'. The scourging
with loaded whips is mentioned by Mark in a single
participle (xv. 15). The mocking by the soldiers which
followed is told more fully. Jesus was clothed with a
purple cloak and crowned with a chaplet of thorns which
with much justice has recently been described as 'a
caricature of the radiate crown of the divine ruler'.[1] The
soldiers saluted him with the words, 'Hail, King of the
Jews!', struck his head with a reed, spat upon him, and
knelt in mock homage before him (Mk. xv. 16–20). A
similar story is told by Luke of Herod's soldiers, which
many scholars believe to be a variant of the Markan
narrative, though Streeter gives good reasons for accepting it as genuine.[2]

It was usual for a condemned man to carry the *pati-
bulum* or cross-beam of his own cross, and John states that
Jesus did this (xix. 17). Mark relates that the soldiers
compelled a man who was passing by, Simon of Cyrene,
to bear it for him (xv. 21), and the most natural explanation of his statement is that Jesus was physically unable
to carry it further. A genuine reminiscence is implied by
Mark's words, for he mentions without explanation that

---

[1] Cf. H. St. J. Hart, *JTS*, N.S., iii. 66–75.
[2] *Oxford Studies in the Synoptic Problem*, 229–31.

Simon was 'coming in from the country' and was 'the father of Alexander and Rufus'. Mark's readers must have known who these men were, and in Rom. xvi. 13 St. Paul mentions a certain Rufus as 'the chosen in the Lord' and refers to his mother as 'his mother and mine', thus suggesting that on some occasion she had shown him 'all the care of a mother, and that therefore he felt for her all the affection of a son'.[1] It cannot be proved that the two men are the same, but since he is connected with the city from which Mark wrote, their identity may reasonably be presumed. Of the identity of Alexander nothing is known, for he cannot have been one of the antagonists of St. Paul mentioned in Ac. xix. 33, I Tim. i. 20 and 2 Tim. iv. 14. Equally with Simon and Rufus it is assumed that he is well known. It is a welcome relief to the tragedy of the story that some of the beholders had compassion on Jesus as he journeyed to the cross. Luke speaks of a great crowd of the people and of women who bewailed and lamented him, to whom he said, 'Daughters of Jerusalem, do not weep for me, but weep for yourselves and your children' (xxiii. 28). These words show that on the *via dolorosa* Jesus was still thinking of the fate of the city and, as the saying which follows shows, in eschatological terms. 'For behold', he said, 'the days are coming, in which they will say, Blessed are the barren, and the wombs that never bore, and the breasts that never gave suck. Then will they begin to say to the mountains, Fall on us; and to the hills, Cover us. For if they do these things in the green tree, what will happen in the dry?' (xxiii. 29–31).

The place of execution was called in Aramaic 'Golgotha' from its resemblance to a skull (Mk. xv. 22, Lk. xxiii. 33). 'And they crucified him'. The dread fact

---

[1] Sanday and Headlam, *Romans*, 427.

P

is recorded as barely as that.   Before crucifixion, in accordance with a merciful Jewish custom, Jesus was offered wine drugged with myrrh, but he refused to drink it choosing to die with an unclouded mind.   In Matthew's later account the influence of Psa. lxix. 2 1[1] is manifest in the statement that the wine was mingled with gall (xxvii. 34).   The fact that the soldiers divided his garments among them by lot reminded the early narrators of Psa. xxii. 18,[2] as Mark's language shows, but the action is so natural that there is no reason to suppose that it was suggested by the Psalm.   Mark expressly notes that it was the third hour, that is, about 9 o'clock in the morning, when Jesus was crucified (xv. 25).[3]   The inscription, 'The King of the Jews', placed according to custom on the cross-beam, is contemptuous in its brevity, and was probably meant by Pilate to satirise the Jews rather than Jesus.   John says that the priests wished it to be altered, but with unexpected firmness Pilate refused, saying, 'What I have written I have written' (xix. 22).

Throughout the accounts of the crucifixion the question constantly arises how far the undoubted interest of the first Christians in the fulfilment of Scripture, and of Psa. xxii in particular, is reflected.   The fact that Jesus expressly quoted this Psalm in the cry, 'My God, my God, why hast thou forsaken me?' (Mk. xv. 34, cf. Psa. xxii. 1), must have drawn their attention to it and have led them to ponder the significance of this and of other Old Testament passages.   On this question one-sided

---

[1] 'They gave me also gall for my meat;  and in my thirst they gave me vinegar to drink'.

[2] 'They part my garments among them, and upon my vesture do they cast lots'.   Jn. xix. 24 cites the LXX verbatim.

[3] C. H. Turner, *op. cit.*, 77, prefers the Western reading in xv. 25, 'they kept watch on him', but the repetition (cf. xv. 24), 'and they crucified him', may be deliberate.

judgements are to be deprecated.  Facts in the Gospel
story will have suggested allusions, and prophecies will
in some cases have coloured details.  These possibilities
will be variously estimated by modern readers.  In
general the signs of Old Testament influence are more
evident in the later Gospel of Matthew.  In Mark and in
Luke the question presses most in the references to the
taunts of the passers-by, the priests, the soldiers, and the
malefactors.  In Mk. xv. 28, which is omitted by the best
manuscripts, later copyists added, 'And the scripture was
fulfilled which says, And he was reckoned with transgressors', probably by assimilation to Lk. xxii. 37.  Mark
itself is least affected by the tendency in question.  The
Evangelist's description of those who passed by and
railed against Jesus, shaking their heads, recalls Lam. ii.
15[1] and Psa. xxii. 7,[2] and it may be that he is influenced
by these passages, but the mockery itself consists of a
repetition of the charge concerning the destruction of the
Temple, 'Aha! You who would destroy the Temple and
build it in three days, save yourself, and come down from
the cross!' (xv. 29).  The mocking of the priests takes up
this taunt in the cry, 'He saved others; himself he cannot
save.  Let the Messiah, the King of Israel, come down
now from the cross, that we may see and believe'(xv. 31f.).
Matthew adds to these derisive words a passage which is
a close approximation to Psa. xxii. 8[3] in the form, 'He
trusts in God; let him deliver him now, if he desires him;
for he said, I am the Son of God' (xxvii. 43).  The only
serious difficulty in the Markan version is the doubt
whether the leading members of the Sanhedrin are likely

---

[1] 'All that pass by . . . shake their head . . .'.
[2] 'All that see me laugh me to scorn: they shoot out the lip, they shake
the head, saying . . .'.
[3] 'Commit thyself unto the Lord; let him deliver him: let him deliver
him, seeing he delighteth in him'.

to have been present in person at the crucifixion; and on this point differences of opinion are possible. We are entitled to infer that a process of dramatisation is increasingly visible in the Synoptic records, and that Mark's account is the most objective of all. Here no taunt at all is uttered by the soldiers and no words are attributed to the bandits who reviled Jesus. In Luke the soldiers cry, 'If you are the King of the Jews, save yourself', and a similar taunt is spoken by one of the malefactors who is immediately rebuked by his companion (xxiii. 36, 39–41).

A more important question concerns the seven sayings from the cross. The Johannine sayings, 'Woman, behold your son!', 'Behold your mother!', 'I thirst', and 'It is finished' (xix. 26–30), illustrate the interpretative purpose which dominates the Fourth Gospel, and will always be of devotional and theological importance for this very reason. *Tetelestai*, 'It is finished', is the magnificent climax of the Johannine narrative, which ends with the majestic words, 'And he bowed his head and gave up his spirit' (xix. 30). In this narrative Jesus dominates the scene throughout. The first of the three Lukan sayings, 'Father, forgive them; for they know not what they do' (xxiii. 34), is wanting in important manuscripts, but it is significant that Hort, who judged it to be a later addition, wrote, 'Few verses of the Gospels bear in themselves a surer witness to the truth of what they record than this first of the Words from the Cross'.[1] Streeter[2] argued that the claim that the saying is an authentic element in the Third Gospel deserves serious consideration and quotes with approval the suggestion of J. Rendel Harris, that the passage was deleted because some Christian in the second century found it hard to believe that God could or

[1] *The New Testament in the Original Greek*, Appendix, 68.
[2] *The Four Gospels*, 138f.

ought to forgive the Jews. Recently W. L. Knox[1] has
expressed the same view. The remaining Lukan sayings,
'Truly, I tell you, to-day you will be with me in Paradise'
(xxiii. 43), spoken to the penitent bandit, and 'Father,
into thy hands I commit my spirit' (xxiii. 46), are
derived from Luke's special source (L) and may be
primitive homiletical expansions of the original tradition.

The most challenging, and the most difficult, of the
seven sayings is the single example given by Mark.
Mark records that after the darkness, which lasted from
midday until 3 o'clock in the afternoon, Jesus cried with a
loud voice, '*Eloi, Eloi, lama sabachthani?*', that is, 'My
God, my God, why hast thou forsaken me?' (xv. 34).
Nowhere are attempts to explain any saying as 'a com-
munity-product' so thin and unconvincing. A saying
recognised as genuine by such radical critics as P. W.
Schmiedel, Arno Neumann, and Joseph Klausner is not
likely to be an invention. W. L. Knox[2] observes that
the view that it is due to the imagination of the source, as
a proof of the fulfilment in Jesus of the Messianic Psa.
xxii, 'deserves to be regarded as one of the most remarkable curiosities of criticism'. 'There could never have
been a moment when Jesus was regarded as the risen
Lord, and yet credited with the utterance of such a cry'.
The theological implications of the saying present a
difficult problem. The explanation that Jesus was
abandoned by the Father and endured the punishment of
the lost no longer merits discussion. The opposite interpretation, widely received as it has been in modern times,
that, as the opening verse of a Psalm which breathes the
spirit of trust, the saying expresses faith rather than
despair, is a feeble reaction against older and obsolete

---

[1] *The Sources of the Synoptic Gospels*, i. 146.
[2] *Op. cit.*, i. 146.

views.  D. F. Strauss[1] made a pertinent comment on this exegesis when he observed that, if the cry is a declaration of faith, it is singular that Jesus should quote the means the least adapted to his purpose.  The best alternative, I believe, is to recognise that the saying expresses a feeling of utter desolation of spirit, a sense of abandonment and momentary despair.  T. R. Glover[2] has finely observed that there never was an utterance that reveals more amazingly the distance between feeling and fact.  Jesus felt the horror of sin so deeply that for a time the closeness of his communion with the Father was obscured.

Mark relates that some of the bystanders thought that Jesus was calling for Elijah, and that one ran, and putting a sponge full of vinegar on a reed, sought to give him to drink, saying, 'Let us see if Elijah will come to take him down' (xv. 36).  It may be that the man was a compassionate soldier, and that Matthew is right in attributing the words to the other bystanders (Mt. xxvii. 49), but naturally on a point of this kind certainty is not possible.  The statement that the veil of the Temple was torn from the top to the bottom (Mk. xv. 38) is probably doctrinal in origin, expressing the view that the way to God is opened by the death of Christ and the Temple system ended.  The alternative is to regard it as a prodigy like the other legendary details which Matthew adds, the rending of the rocks, the opening of the tombs, and the rising of dead saints (Mt. xxvii. 51–3).

The death of Jesus is described by Mark with the utmost simplicity.  'Jesus', he writes, 'uttered a loud cry and breathed his last' (xv. 37).  Probably the Authorized Version is right in suggesting that it was the loud cry of Jesus which riveted the centurion's attention as he stood

[1] *The Life of Jesus*, 688.
[2] *The Jesus of History*, 192.

facing the cross: 'When the centurion, which stood over against him, saw that he so cried out, and gave up the ghost, he said, Truly this man was the Son of God' (Mk. xv. 39).[1]  The centurion himself may have used the term 'son of God' in the pagan sense, as a spontaneous recognition of divinity in a man of outstanding greatness,[2] or it may be that Luke's version, 'a righteous man' (xxiii. 47), is more primitive.  Mark, however, reads into his words the deepest secret of the person of Christ, and intends his confession at the end of his Gospel to match his opening words, 'Here begins the Gospel of Jesus Christ, the Son of God', at the beginning.  At a distance, looking on from afar, stood Mary Magdalene, Mary the mother of James the less and Joses, and Salome, who is identified by Matthew with the mother of the sons of Zebedee, together with other women who had come up with Jesus to Jerusalem (Mk. xv. 40f.).  The reference to them forms an introduction to the narratives of the Burial and the Resurrection.

[1] So RVmg and RSVmg.  For the textual problem cf. V. Taylor, *The Gospel according to St. Mark*, 597.
[2] Cf. RVmg and RSV.

# LI

## THE BURIAL

FROM the earliest times the fact that Jesus died, was buried, and rose again was emphasised, as I Cor. xv. 3–7 shows, in Christian credal confessions. The story of the burial is detailed and full of movement. It was now late in the afternoon, and the Sabbath, which began at sunset, was hastening on. It was necessary therefore to act with speed. The initiative was taken by Joseph of Arimathaea, who is described by Mark as an influential councillor, that is, presumably, a member of the Sanhedrin, who looked for the fulfilment of the Messianic hope of Israel. He is not said by Mark to have been a disciple, although later Matthew describes him as such (xxvii. 57). Luke speaks of him as 'a good and righteous man' who had not consented to the purpose and deed of the council (xxiii. 50f.). Apparently, his action was dictated by sympathy with Jesus, piety towards those who were executed, and concern for ritual purity. It was usual for the bodies of the crucified to be left hanging upon the crosses, but it was also in accordance with custom to hand them over to friends and relatives for burial if permission was sought and obtained. Taking his courage into his hands, Joseph went in to Pilate and asked for the body of Jesus. Pilate was astonished that Jesus had died so quickly, but when he was assured by the centurion that he was dead already, he freely granted the corpse to Joseph. The Greek phrase has a legal ring, and, as Rawlinson[1] has suggested, may perhaps render the official wording of

[1] *The Gospel according to St. Mark,* 241.

the governor's permission, *donavit cadaver*. Having bought a linen shroud, he took Jesus down from the cross, and wrapping him in the cloth, laid him in a rock-tomb, and in the stark words of the record, rolled a stone against the door of the tomb. No disciple was present, but Mary Magdalene and Mary the mother of Joses saw where he was laid. No reference is made to anointing. In this matter we must infer that Mark's silence was intentional, since he explains the purpose of the women at the tomb on the third day as that of anointing (xvi. 1), and probably interpreted literally the words of Jesus to the woman at Bethany, 'She has anointed my body beforehand for burying' (xiv. 8). The same silence is observed by Matthew (xxvii. 60) and by Luke (xxiii. 53), who further says that the women returned and prepared spices and ointment (xxiii. 56). We must prefer these accounts to that of John who follows a tradition in which the familiar offices were fulfilled (xix. 39f.).[1] A hurried burial by strangers, Joseph and presumably his servants, in a rock-tomb,[2] with no others present save the women, and with only the barest of necessary funeral customs, is the picture we gain from the earliest tradition. We rightly make much of the empty tomb, but we have not done justice to the objectivity of the primitive record unless we think also of the closed tomb and hear the great stone rolling against its door. Here truly do we see the reality of the humanity of Jesus who, as the Creed says, 'suffered and was buried'.

[1] Attempts to reconcile the variant traditions by combining both are surely to be deprecated.

[2] The later Gospels speak of it as Joseph's 'own new tomb' (Mt. xxvii. 60) and as 'a new tomb where no one had ever been laid' (Jn. xix. 41, cf. Lk. xxiii. 53). Luke appears to think of a tomb built of hewn stones, but J.M. Creed, *The Gospel according to St. Luke*, 292, thinks that probably he had no intention of conveying a meaning different from that of Mark. Rock-tombs were common, sometimes containing chambers and sometimes a single chamber with a bench or shelf on which the body was laid.

# LII

## THE RESURRECTION

No one who has followed carefully the detailed and continuous Passion Narratives in the Gospels can fail to be struck by the fragmentary character of the Resurrection stories. Each is aflame with the Resurrection message, 'He is risen', but it is quite impossible to weave them into a whole, so as to give a sustained account of the successive appearances of Jesus to his disciples, with precise references to time and place and the careful distinction of one narrative from another. Well meant attempts to harmonise the narratives by the aid of ingenious, but not convincing, speculations, only serve to bring historical criticism into disrepute, and it is wise neither to attempt nor to entertain them. I am convinced that the best explanation of the broken character of the tradition is the one I gave some years ago now in *The Formation of the Gospel Tradition* (1933),[1] namely, that, while from the first it was necessary to tell the Passion Story as a whole, in order to explain how Jesus came to be crucified by the Jews, the immediate need in the case of the Resurrection was 'assurance about a new and astounding fact', the truth that Jesus was risen and had appeared to his disciples from the third day onwards. When at length the time came to co-ordinate the original facts in the Gospels, the Evangelists could do no more than record the local traditions of the Churches for which they wrote, traditions which vary in historical value and cannot in all points be reconciled. Some of the

[1] 2nd ed. (1935), 59–62.

narratives contain legendary details, as, for example, when the Risen Christ is said to have eaten a piece of broiled fish (Lk. xxiv. 42); while others are products of conscious art, based upon tradition, as in the story of the journey to Emmaus (Lk. xxiv. 13–35), and the Johannine narratives of Mary Magdalene in the garden (Jn. xx. 11–18), of Thomas (Jn. xx. 19–29), and the Appearance by the sea of Tiberias (Jn. xxi. 1–14).

The Markan story of the Visit of the Women to the Tomb (xvi. 1–8) is one which had been told at Rome when interest in the Empty Tomb had quickened. The strange statement that the women fled from the tomb and 'said nothing to any one, for they were afraid' (xvi. 8), appears to suggest that the story had not been known earlier, while the motive of anointing given for the visit, the question about the stone, the description of the young man who is probably an angel, and his verbal message suggest a reverent reconstruction of the incident for catechetical purposes. Such a critical estimate in no way compromises the fact of the Resurrection, nor is it necessarily inconsistent with belief in the empty Tomb; it is merely a tentative historical judgement concerning the earliest available narrative.

The Resurrection narratives will always focus and quicken Christian belief, but they are not the primary basis of that belief. The historical arguments for the Resurrection are what they have always been, the immense change in the first disciples wrought by their knowledge of the Risen Lord, the conversion and life of the Apostle Paul, and the existence and continued life of the Christian Church. Coupled with these historical arguments is the living experience of the individual Christian believer of fellowship with the Risen Christ. The weight of Scriptural teaching is to be found in the

224 THE LIFE AND MINISTRY OF JESUS

primitive records of Christian preaching contained in the early chapters of the Acts of the Apostles (ii. 24, 32, iii. 15, iv. 10, v. 31) and in the testimony of the Epistles, especially that of St. Paul in I Cor. xv. From the day of Pentecost onwards the first preachers proclaimed that God had raised up Jesus, 'whereof', they said, 'we all are witnesses' (Ac. ii. 32, iii. 15). 'Him', they declared, 'did God exalt with his right hand to be a Pioneer and a Saviour, to give repentance to Israel, and remission of sins' (Ac. v. 31). St. Paul set in the foreground of his teaching the fact that Christ 'was declared to be the Son of God with power, according to the spirit of holiness, by the resurrection of the dead' (Rom. i. 4), and St. Peter exulted in the great mercy of the Father who 'begat us again unto a living hope by the resurrection of Jesus Christ from the dead' (I Pet. i. 3). The liturgical statement of I Cor. xv. 3–7 is earlier than St. Paul himself, bearing as it does all the signs of being an extract from a primitive Christian creed, and therefore separated from the basic facts by less than the period of twenty-five years of which apologists have been wont to speak. 'For I delivered to you', he writes, 'as of first importance what I also received, that Christ died for our sins in accordance with the scriptures, that he was buried, that he was raised on the third day in accordance with the scriptures, and that he appeared to Cephas, then to the twelve. Then he appeared to more than five hundred brethren at once, most of whom are still alive, though some have fallen asleep. Then he appeared to James, then to all the apostles'. 'Last of all', St. Paul adds, 'as to one untimely born, he appeared also to me'.

'Why is it judged incredible with you', St. Paul is reported to have asked King Agrippa, 'that God raises the dead?' (Ac. xxvi. 8). To this question we may reply, it is

not incredible at all, as the climax of the life of Jesus
Christ, as he is presented to us in the Gospels, and as he was
described by the first preachers.   All the emphasis was
laid on the fact that God raised him from the dead and that
he had appeared to chosen witnesses.   The belief concerning the empty tomb was assumed from the beginning,
probably by St. Paul himself, but apparently it was not a
theme of first interest in the earliest preaching.   From
St. Paul's teaching in I Cor. xv. 35–58 we may infer that
the resurrection-body of the Lord was transformed so that
it became 'a spiritual body', fitted to be the organ of his
risen life, and with this view those elements in the
Gospel narratives which speak of his sudden appearances
and departures, even when the doors were shut (Jn. xx.
19, 26, cf. Lk. xxiv. 31), are in full agreement.   But the
precise nature of the body, as well as the character of the
appearances themselves, remain matters for reverent
speculation, since so much is hidden from us.   No obliga-
tion is imposed upon us either to ignore the difficulties of
the Resurrection narratives or to attempt to explain them
away.   What must be insisted upon is that they are not
of first importance, since belief in the Risen Christ has
better foundations.   The Christ whose story we have
sought to recall, Son of Man and Son of God, who believed that his suffering was necessary for the salvation of
men, is one for whom death could not be the end.   As St.
Peter truly said 'it was not possible that he should be
holden of it' (Ac. ii. 24).   With no less confidence,
although without knowledge of when or how, must the
Church look for his appearing, answering the challenge,
*Sursum Corda*, 'Lift up your hearts', with the glad reply,
'We lift them up to the Lord'.

# INDEX OF SCRIPTURE PASSAGES

# INDEX OF PROPER NAMES

PRINTED IN GREAT BRITAIN BY ROBERT MACLEHOSE AND CO. LTD
THE UNIVERSITY PRESS, GLASGOW